# NOTES:

*I dedicate my 1st "Just Shut Up and Eat It" Cookbook to my Grandma Margaret Howard.*

*My Grandma taught me how to love, cook, bake, sew, create crafts
& how to work hard for what you believe.*

*Grandma raised 4 wonderful people, my Mom, Roberta Lindenberg, my Uncle
& Godfather, Robert B. Campbell, Aunt Ruth Pratnicki & my Aunt Jean Dobozy.*

*Grandma, my Mom & Aunts have walked on from this earth
and have left us their legacy of how important family is.*

*I am grateful for the love you all shared with so many.
I am thankful for my favorite brother, Eric, my favorite sister, Katy Salutes,
my awesome Nephews, Nieces, my Cousins, my Sons, Josh, Jeremy (& Kera).
My Grandson, Chef Riley, who is learning the things
Grandma taught me all those years ago.*

*Uncle Bob, thank you for all you have done for me and the wisdom you still share.*

*My deepest gratitude to John Colley and Linda Williamson,
who without their help, this cookbook would not have been possible.*

Don Gallatin from Birch Run, MI.
Walking the Mackinac Bridge on Labor Day 2012

**We live in a society where pizza gets to your house before the police.   3**

Men have two emotions: Hungry and horny. If you see he's tired, make him a sandwich.

# Table of Contents

We never really grow up, we only learn how to eat in public.

Here's Bill Lowe
from Trollville ~
Bill says the grill won't start
without a cold beer on hand.

Going to church doesn't make you a Christian any more than standing in a kitchen makes you a cook.

# OLDE WORLD CRANBERRY NUT BREAD

*by Kyle Cork AuTrain, MI*

1 cup milk (80 degrees)
2 Tbsp. canola oil
¾ cup beet sugar
1 tsp. cinnamon (fresh ground)
1 tsp. sea salt
¾ cup dried course chopped cranberries
1/4 cup dried course chopped cherries

1 egg (room temperature)
2 ½ cups unbleached all purpose flour
1 Tbsp. dark brown sugar
3 ½ tsp. baking powder

1 cup walnuts (hand crushed)

Mix all ingredients well. Pour in non stick or lightly oiled loaf pan. Bake at 350° for 45 minutes or until done. Check with toothpick.

# SHREDDED WHEAT BREAD

*Submitted by Tator O'Connor • Lebanon, PA*

2 cups boiling water
1 tsp. salt
1/3 cup sugar
2 Shredded Wheat Biscuits (crushed up)
3 Tbsp. shortening

Mix above ingredients and let them get mushy and cool a bit.

**Dissolve 1 pkg. yeast in 1/2 cup warm water with 1 tsp. sugar and a pinch of soda.**

**Add:**

**1/2 cup molasses and yeast mixture**

**Add:**

**5 - 6 cups flour**

Combine all, mix and knead until smooth. Place in a greased bowl, let rise, punch down. Divide in half. Place into 2- 9 x 5 bread pans. Bake at 350° degrees for 1/2 hour.

Slather with butter when done. Makes 2 loaves.

**Do not argue with a bad cook. He will drag you down to his level and beat you with experience.**   7

# PISTACHIO BREAD
*Submitted by Joann Schmidt - Chesaning, MI*

1 yellow cake mix
4 eggs
1 small box instant pistachio dry pudding
1/4 cup oil
1/4 cup water
1/2 pint sour cream

Mix all ingredients above. Grease 2 bread pans. Pour half of the batter into each pan. Sprinkle batter with cinnamon and sugar. Then pour remaining batter into both pans and sprinkle top with more cinnamon and sugar. Bake 325° for 30 to 40 minutes.

# LEMON BREAD
*Submitted by Joann Schmidt - Chesaning, MI*

1 pkg. white or yellow cake mix
4 eggs
1/2 pint sour cream
1/4 cup oil
1/2 cup water
1 pkg. instant lemon pudding (or use 1 package lemon cake mix and 1 package of vanilla instant pudding.) I prefer using Lemon Cake mix.

## Topping:
1 cup brown sugar
1 tsp. cinnamon
1 tsp. ginger
1/4 tsp. nutmeg

Mix first 6 ingredients. Divide batter in half. Place in greased pans. Sprinkle topping mix on batter and then put rest of batter in and sprinkle on top. Bake 350° for 45 to 50 minutes.

8     **The last thing I want to do is poison you. But it's still on the list.**

# EASY APPLE BREAD

*In Memory of Karen Black*

## Bread:

1/2 cup shortening or butter
1 cup sugar
2 eggs
2 tsp. milk
1 tsp. vanilla
2 cup flour
2 tsp. baking powder
1/8 tsp. salt
1 cup chopped apples
1/4 cup chopped nuts

Cream shortening, add sugar gradually. Cream until light and fluffy. Add salt and vanilla, mix well.

Add eggs and beat well. Add milk, apples, and nuts, mix well again. Add flour and baking powder, which has been sifted together. Stir well, pour into well greased loaf pan. Bake at 350° degrees for 50-60 minutes. Remove and cool well. Prepare glaze below and pour over bread.

## Glaze:

1/2 cup sifted powdered sugar          1 Tbsp. water
2 Tbsp. butter

Mix well and pour over bread, let it drizzle down the sides. Wrap in plastic and store 24 hours before slicing.

# MORNING GLORY MUFFINS

*THE COMBINATION OF FRUIT AND NUTS MAKES these muffins from Nantucket's Morning Glory Café a wonderful breakfast treat.*

2 ½ cups sugar
4 cups flour
4 teaspoons cinnamon
4 teaspoons baking soda
1 teaspoons salt
1 cup raisins, plumped in brandy and drained
1 cup coconut, shredded
4 cups shredded carrots
2 apples, shredded
1 cup pecans
6 eggs
2 cups vegetable oil
1 teaspoon vanilla extract

Heat oven to 375°. Sift dry ingredients into a large bowl. Lightly dust the raisins with flour. Add the coconut, carrots, fruit, and nuts, and stir well. Add the eggs, oil, and vanilla, stirring only until combined.

Spoon batter in cupcake tins and bake for 20 minutes. Muffins should "ripen" for 24 hours for maximum blending of flavors.

MAKES 16–20 MUFFINS

**Knowledge is knowing a tomato is a fruit; Wisdom is not putting it in a fruit salad.**

# BOARDINGHOUSE-STYLE BISCUITS

*Mrs. Wilkes' serves about 630 biscuits a day. The Wilkes' family loves these with Georgia cane syrup, and eats them morning, noon, and night – even as dessert!*

**2 cups self-rising flour**　　　　**½ teaspoon baking powder**
**1 teaspoon sugar**　　　　　　　**2 tablespoons shortening**
**2 tablespoons butter or margarine**
**1/3 cup buttermilk**　　　　　　**1/3 cup whole milk**
**1 tablespoon plus 1 teaspoon water**

　　Preheat the oven to 450°. Grease an 8 by 8 by 2-inch baking pan well. Sift the flour, baking powder, and sugar into a bowl. Cut in the shortening and butter until the mixture resembles coarse cornmeal. Make a well in the center of the flour and pour in the buttermilk and milk. Mix lightly and quickly with your hands to form a dough moist enough to leave the sides of the bowl. If too dry add water a little at a time. Turn onto a lightly floured surface. Knead by picking up the sides of the dough away from you while pressing down with the palms of your hands and pushing the dough away. Repeat 6 or 7 times. Work the dough into a large ball while kneading. Keep your fingers dry by frequently dipping them in dry flour. Pinch off portions of dough for desired size biscuit. Press lightly to make the biscuits look flat on the pan. Make sure the biscuits touch each other. Bake for 15 minutes. Yields about 8 boardinghouse-sized biscuits.

# HUCKLEBERRY MUFFINS

2 cups flour
3 teaspoons baking powder
¾ cup sugar
1 teaspoon salt
1/4 cup shortening
2 eggs (beaten)
1 cup milk
1 cup huckleberries

Sift together all dry ingredients. Blend in shortening and add eggs. Add remaining ingredients using as few strokes as possible. Fold in huckleberries last. Fill greased muffin pans 2/3 full.
Bake 400° – 25 minutes. Makes 10-12 muffins.
Blueberries may be substituted.

# TO DIE FOR BLUEBERRY MUFFINS

1 1/2 cups all-purpose flour
3/4 cup white sugar
1/2 teaspoon salt
2 teaspoons baking powder
1/3 cup vegetable oil
1 egg
1/3 cup milk
1 cup fresh blueberries
1/2 cup white sugar
1/3 cup all-purpose flour
1/4 cup butter, cubed
1 1/2 teaspoons ground cinnamon

1. Preheat oven to 400 degrees F (200 degrees C). Grease muffin cups or line with muffin liners.

2. Combine 1 1/2 cups flour, 3/4 cup sugar, salt and baking powder. Place vegetable oil into a 1 cup measuring cup; add the egg and enough milk to fill the cup. Mix this with flour mixture. Fold in blueberries. Fill muffin cups right to the top, and sprinkle with crumb topping mixture.

3. *To Make Crumb Topping:* Mix together 1/2 cup sugar, 1/3 cup flour, 1/4 cup butter, and 1 1/2 teaspoons cinnamon. Mix with fork, and sprinkle over muffins before baking.

4. Bake for 20 to 25 minutes in the preheated oven, or until done. - *Blueberry photo by Penny Smith*

(Grandma Puppies)

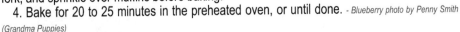

**To steal recipes from one person is plagiarism. To steal from many is research.**

# HUSHPUPPIES

*From Hudson's Dock on Hilton Head Island*

2 lbs. cornmeal
3 tablespoons baking powder
6 tablespoons sugar
1/2 cup salad oil
1 cup buttermilk
1 lb. flour
3 tablespoons salt
5 tablespoons parsley
8 eggs (lightly beaten)
1 cup dehydrated onion flakes

Mix all ingredients well. Spoon into small balls and deep fry until golden brown and crusty on the outside.

Yields 35-50

**If God is watching us, the least we can do is be entertaining.**

# CAKE MIX CINNAMON ROLLS

*Bobbie@Settler's Co-op Bruce Crossing • Yield: 16 rolls*

*This recipe is absolutely delicious. I make them the night before, take them out in the morning and let them rise. I have also made sticky buns with this recipe using a coconut/pecan frosting for the bottom of my pan.*

## INGREDIENTS:

3 (.25 ounces) packages active dry yeast
2 ½ cups warm water
1 (18.25 ounce) package white cake mix
4 ½ cups all-purpose flour
½ cup butter, softened
½ cup brown sugar
2 teaspoons ground cinnamon
¼ cup butter, melted
1/3 cup white sugar

## DIRECTIONS:

1. In a small bowl, dissolve yeast in warm water. Let stand until creamy, about 10 minutes.

2. In a large bowl, combine the yeast mixture with the cake mix and 3 cups of the flour; stir to combine. Add the remaining flour, ½ cup at a time, stirring well after each addition. When the dough has pulled together, turn it out onto a lightly floured surface and knead until smooth and elastic, about 8 minutes.

3. Lightly oil a large bowl, place the dough in the bowl and turn to coat with oil. Cover with a damp cloth and let rise in a warm place until doubled in volume, about 30 minutes.

4. Deflate the dough and turn it out onto a lightly floured surface. Roll the dough into a 10x16 inch rectangle. Spread the softened butter over the rectangle; sprinkle on brown sugar and cinnamon. Starting from one of the long sides, roll up the rectangle and cut into 1 inch wide rolls.

5. Preheat oven to 375 degrees F (190 degrees C). Grease a 9x13 inch baking pan. Pour the melted butter into a small bowl and mix the white sugar and 1/2 cup pecans (optional) in another small bowl. Dip the top of each roll in the melted butter, then in the sugar and pecan mixture, then place the topped rolls snugly into the prepared pan. Cover the rolls with a damp cloth and let rise until doubled in volume, about 30 minutes.

6. Bake at 375 degrees F (190 degrees C) for 20 minutes, or until rolls are golden.

**If you think nobody thinks your a good cook, let them miss a couple of meals.**     13

# Chef Riley & Chef Dennis Present - EASY STICKY BUNS

A surprise visit by Chef Riley resulted in some great fun and together we baked up a delicious batch of my Easy Sticky Buns. As you can see young Chef Riley assisted at each step. It's a great recipe to make together with your own youngsters at home.

What makes this recipe so easy is that you use packaged puff pastry dough instead of bread dough. And you still get all that ooey gooey sweet caramel sticky goodness. Personally, I like the lighter flakier texture of puff pastry rather than the heavier and chewy texture of traditional bread dough varieties. The whole process goes a lot quicker too. No need to wait for the dough to rise. I always keep a package of puff pastry handy in my freezer. It's inexpensive, thaws quickly and keeps well in the refrigerator. Best of all, puff pastry can be handled quite easily by young chefs with some adult supervision.

**IMPORTANT NOTE:** While phyllo (or filo) dough and puff pastry dough may seem very similar, they are made differently and are **NOT** interchangeable in this recipe. Phyllo dough is tissue-thin pastry used in many Greek and Middle Eastern dishes, such as baklava. It dries out quickly and rips easily so working with it requires more care. Individual sheets of phyllo are assembled with brushed butter or oil between the layers. I've previously shown you how to use phyllo dough to make my Chicken En Croute and Stuffed Mushroom Kisses.

Puff pastry, whether homemade or store-bought, has a richer and less fragile texture. It rises (puffs) more when baked. It is made by placing chilled butter between layers of pastry dough, then rolled out, folded, allowed to rest and the process repeated another six to eight times. Each sheet then of finished puff pastry is thicker than the individual sheets of phyllo. While some home cooks enjoy making puff pastry from scratch, making phyllo dough is extremely complicated and time-consuming and best left to commercial bakeries.

I usually double this recipe when I make it. Ingredients and instructions below are for a single batch. Feel free to adjust the spices a bit. For instance, my wife loves to add a pinch of ground cloves or allspice. You can also substitute nuts, but personally a sticky bun just isn't the same without pecans. The recipe is pretty straight forward. You first cream the butter and sugar and spoon it into the bottom of your muffin tins and top with pecans. Then add the pieces of cut rolled dough. The butter, sugar, & pecan mix will caramalize during baking and seep into the crevices of the baked puff pastry when you flip the pan over to release the buns. Take care not to overbake the buns. They can quickly go from almost done to burnt during the last minute or so, and you might not be able to tell until you've flipped them out to cool.

# Ingredients for Sticky Caramel Mixture

12 tablespoons (1 ½ sticks) butter (salted or unsalted), at room temperature
½ cup light brown sugar, lightly packed
2/3 cup pecans, chopped in large pieces

# Ingredients for puff pastry filling

2 tablespoons butter,
   melted and cooled
2/3 cup light brown
   sugar, lightly packed
¼ cup ground cinnamon
1/8 teaspoon ground
   nutmeg (optional)
1 cup raisins (optional)
Puff pastry dough
1 package (17.3 ounces/
   2-sheets) frozen puff
   pastry, defrosted

# Directions

Preheat the oven to 400 degrees F. Place a 12 cup standard muffin tin on a sheet pan lined with parchment paper. Note: The parchment paper is optional but makes cleanup easier. You can substitute waxed paper.

While the oven is preheating, cream the butter and brown sugar well for the sticky caramel. Use the paddle attachment with your stand mixer or regular beaters if using a hand-mixer. Place 1 rounded tablespoon of the mixture in each of the 12 muffin tin cups. Divide the pecans evenly on top of the butter and sugar (caramel) mixture.

Lightly flour a wooden board or pastry work surface. Unfold 1 sheet of puff pastry with the folds going left to right. Brush the whole sheet gently with the melted butter. Sprinke the sheet with half of filling mixture, leaving a 1-inch border on the puff pastry. TIP: Combine the filling sugar and spices and store in a container with a shaker top. Starting with the end nearest you, roll the pastry up snugly like a jelly roll, finishing with the seam side down. Trim about ½ inch off each end and discard. Slice the roll into 6 equal pieces, each about 1 ½ inches wide. Place each piece, spiral side up, on top of the caramal pecans mixture already in the tins. Repeat with the second sheet of puff pastry to make 12 sticky buns.

Bake for 35-40 minutes, until the sticky buns are golden to dark brown on top and firm to the touch. Be careful! They will be hot! Allow to cool for 5 minutes only, and then invert the buns onto the parchment paper. You can ease the caramel and pecans out onto the buns with a spoon. Cool completely.

**Dolphins are so smart that within a few weeks, they can train people to throw them fish.**

# PIÑA COLADA BREAD

Ingredients:

½ cup butter (1 stick), softened
1 cup sugar
3 eggs
1 teaspoon vanilla extract
¼ cup rum (dark preferred)
½ cup cream of coconut
3 cups crushed pineapple

●●●●

2 ¼ cups all-purpose flour
1 tablespoon baking powder
1 teaspoon baking soda
1 teaspoon salt
1 cup coconut
   (medium flake)

Directions:

Cream the butter and sugar.
Add the eggs, vanilla, rum,
cream of coconut, and pineapple.
Mix the dry ingredients. Add
to the wet mixture. Pour into
a well-greased loaf pan. Bake
in a 350° oven for 1 hour, or
until it tests done.
Makes 1 loaf.

I thought I wanted to be a chef, turns out I just wanted paychecks.

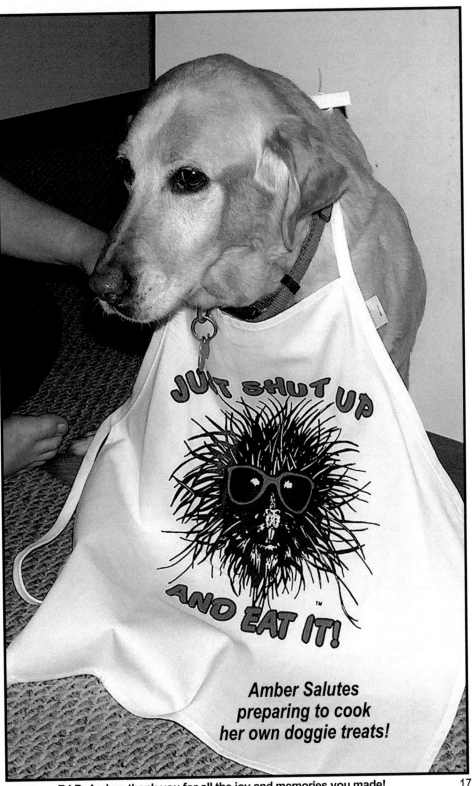

Amber Salutes
preparing to cook
her own doggie treats!

R.I.P. Amber, thank you for all the joy and memories you made!

# PUFFY OVEN APPLE PANCAKE

### Pancake

1 1/2 cups all-purpose flour
6 large eggs
1 teaspoon salt

1 1/2 cups milk
1 tablespoon sugar
1/2 cup (1 stick) butter

### Apple Filling

2 large Golden Delicious or Granny Smith Apples, peeled and sliced
2 tablespoons butter
1/4 cup light or dark brown sugar
Whipped cream for serving (optional)

To make pancake: In a bowl, whisk together flour, milk, eggs, sugar and salt until no lumps remain. Let stand for 30 minutes. (You can mix batter the night before, cover and refrigerate. Remove from refrigerator when you begin preheating oven.)

Preheat oven to 450°F. While oven preheats, place a large slope-sided baking pan or ovenproof skillet into oven and add butter. When butter is melted, remove from oven.

Pour pancake mixture into heated pan and return to oven. Bake pancake for 15 to 20 minutes, until edges are puffed high and golden.

To make apple filling: While pancake bakes, in medium skillet, sauté apples in butter until tender, 5 to 10 minutes. Add brown sugar and stir until dissolved. Transfer to serving bowl.

To serve pancake, be sure guests are at the table when you bring it in, as it will slump quickly. Cut pancake into quarters, and fill each serving with sautéed apples. Pass the whipped cream on the side, if desired. - Serves 4

# EASY BREAKFAST FOR 6 TO 8

*Donna Nugent*

3 cup milk
1/2 tsp. onion powder
1/4 tsp. pepper
1 tsp. Worcestershire sauce
1 tsp. brown sugar
1/2 lb. ham
1/2 lb. shredded cheese

1/4 tsp. paprika
1 tsp. salt
1/8 tsp. cayenne
1 tsp. dry mustard
14 pieces of bread (no crusts)
8 eggs

Combine liquids and spices in pouring container. Layer half the bread, ham, and cheese in a 9x13x2" baking dish (spray dish). Repeat layering bread, ham, and cheese. Beat eggs into liquid mixture. Pour over bread, ham, and cheese. Refrigerate overnight if desired. Bake at 350° for 1 hour. Remove and let set for 10 minutes.

**I didn't fight my way to the top of the food chain to be a vegetarian.**

# BLUEBERRY STUFFED FRENCH TOAST

*Sheryl Horetski*

**12 slices thick hearty white bread, cut into 1" cubes**
**2-8 oz. pkgs. cream cheese, cut into 1" cubes**
**2 cup blueberries**
**12 eggs**
**1/3 cup maple syrup**
**2 cup milk**
**1 cup sugar**
**2 Tbsp. cornstarch**
**1 cup water**
**1 Tbsp. butter**
**1 tsp. cinnamon**

Arrange half the bread cubes in a buttered 9x13" pan. Scatter cream cheese over bread and sprinkle 1 cup blueberries over cream cheese. Top with remaining bread cubes. In large bowl, whisk eggs, syrup and milk; stir in cinnamon. Pour over bread. Cover and refrigerate overnight. Remove from refrigerator; let stand for 30 minutes. Bake at 350° for 30 minutes. Uncover & bake another 30 minutes. While baking, combine sugar and cornstarch in saucepan; stir in water. Cook over medium heat until thickened. Stir in 1 cup blueberries and cook about 10 minutes. Remove from heat and stir in butter. Serve sauce over the "French Toast."

**I didn't say the bad meal was your fault, I said I was blaming you.** 19

## SAUSAGE- N- PANCAKES

*Pancakes & sausage are 2 of my favorite foods. Together they're delicious!*

*Have your adult cook sausage links, set aside.*

Cook pancake (using a mix) so it is longer than it is wide, place cooked pancake on plate, place sausage link on & roll it up. Set seam side down. (tip: for easier to roll pancakes, add a little extra water to the mix)

Pour on the syrup & sprinkle on some powdered sugar.

*We used a peach cobbler syrup or you can use maple, blueberry syrup or jelly.*

*Hope you like them! - Photos by Robin Lindenberg*

## GRANDMA ALLIE'S POTATO PANCAKES

*Marta Bostic*
*An heirloom recipe.*
*Serve with Applesauce & Sour Cream*

Ingredients:

3 cup peeled, finely grated white potatoes

1 Tbsp. grated onion

1 egg

1 tsp. salt

1/8 tsp. pepper

5 Tbsp. Southern Breakfast pancake mix

*Directions:*

Plan to make and fry pancakes immediately after preparing potatoes to prevent darkening. To the grated potatoes, add onion, egg, seasonings and pancake mix. Mix well. Drop by tablespoonfuls into hot fat, 1/2 – inch deep. Fry until crisp and golden brown on underside: turn and brown remaining side. Drain. Serve while hot.

Yields 16 pancakes.

**The voices in my head may not be real, but they have some good ideas!**

# GUEST PLEASIN' ÆBELSKIVERS

**3 eggs, separated**
**2 cups buttermilk**
**2 cups all-purpose flour**
**3 tablespoons sugar**
**1 teaspoon baking soda**
**1/2 teaspoon salt**
**1 teaspoon baking powder**
**Shortening**

Beat the egg yolks and add the buttermilk. Add the dry ingredients gradually, beating well. Beat the egg whites until stiff and fold them into the other mixture. Melt 1/4 teaspoon shortening in each cup of an æbelskiver pan and fill each with batter. Cook until bubbly, then turn with a sharp instrument (we use an ice pick). Keep rotating it until the toothpick test shows they are fully cooked. Serve with preserves, syrup or honey butter. You may also cook with pieces of apple, whole-kernel corn or other fillings in the middle. Simply add the filling before you turn it for the first time.

Makes 2 dozen æbelskivers.

# EGGS BENEDICT FOR TWO

*This elegant dish was a favorite of the King's during his Las Vegas years. It was frequently served to his entourage in his suite at the Las Vegas Hilton, and it was one of the dishes served at the wedding breakfast buffet at the Aladdin Hotel on May 1, 1967. What better musical accompaniment than Viva Las Vegas?*

**1 teaspoon corn oil**
**1 teaspoon white vinegar**
**2 tablespoons butter**
**1 cup milk**
**1 cup shredded Cheddar cheese**
**2 English muffins, split, toasted, and buttered**

**8 slices Canadian bacon**
**4 eggs**
**2 tablespoons flour**

Lightly grease a large frying pan with the corn oil. Heat over medium-high heat. Add the Canadian bacon and cook until well done, about 5 minutes. Drain the bacon on paper toweling. Keep warm.

Bring 2 cups of water to a boil in the bottom of a 4-egg poaching pan. Place ¼ teaspoon vinegar and one egg in each of the cups, and cover. Cook for 2 to 3 minutes. (If you don't have a poaching pan, cook the eggs for 2 to 3 minutes in a small pot of simmering water to which 2 teaspoons of white vinegar has been added.)

While the eggs are cooking, melt the butter in another saucepan. Stir in the flour. Gradually add the milk, stirring constantly. Add cheese, stirring until melted.

Place two slices of Canadian bacon on each English muffin half. Using a slotted spoon, drain the eggs and place poached egg on each muffin.

Pour the cheese sauce over each egg and serve hot.

**A clear conscience is usually the sign of a bad memory.**

Steve Nonnenmacher from Trollville
Looks like Steve is ready to make a
mess in the kitchen!

**Laugh at your baking mistakes, everybody else does.**

# SAUSAGE CORN CHOWDER

*From Coligny Plaza Oceanside on Hilton Head Island*

4 lbs. link sausage
4 dozen ears, sweet corn
1/2 lb. butter
1 large onion, chopped fine
1 cup flour
2 large potatoes, cubed
2 qts. chicken broth
1 qt. heavy cream
1 qt. milk
salt and pepper

On the grill cook sausage, then let it cool. Husk and rinse corn and grill enough to lightly put grill marks on the corn, let cool. In a large pot add butter and onion, cool until translucent. Cut sausage into small cubes, and cut corn from ear. Put into the pot and cook 5 minutes. Now add flour, let cook 5 minutes. Constantly stirring. Add potatoes, chicken stock, cream and milk and bring to a boil stirring. Once thickened add salt and pepper to taste.

# WISCONSIN CHEDDAR CHEESE AND BEER SOUP

*Why put beer in soup? Why not just have a bowl of soup with a beer on the side? You'll find out when you make this.*

4 Tablespoons butter
4 Shallots, minced (About ½ Cup)
4 Tablespoons All-Purpose Flour
4 Cups milk, warmed, divided
1 ½ lbs. Cheddar Cheese, grated
1 Cup beer
1 Teaspoon Curry Powder
1 Teaspoon salt
¼ Teaspoon freshly ground black pepper

1. Heat butter in a large pot. Add shallots and sauté over medium heat for 10 minutes, or until tender. Stir in the flour and cook for 3 to 4 minutes. Whisk in 1 cup of warm milk, stirring constantly until thickened.

2. Slowly add the cheese, ¼ cup at a time, stirring constantly.

3. Whisk in remaining milk and beer. Bring to a boil, whisking until thick.

4. Blend in the curry powder, salt, and pepper.

YIELD: 6 servings • PREPARATION TIME: 15–20 minutes • COOKING TIME: 25–30 minutes

**He who smiles when the smoke clears in the kitchen has found someone to blame.**

# CORN CHOWDER

*Submitted by Tom & Tator O'Connor • Lebanon, PA*

4-6 slices bacon, fried and crumbled
4-6 small potatoes, cubed
1 small onion, chopped
2- 15 oz. cans of corn - drained
2- 15 oz. creamed cans of corn
1- 12 oz. can evaporated milk plus
1- 5 oz. can
salt and pepper to taste

In dutch oven cook bacon until crisp. Remove and drain. Sauté onion and add potatoes.

Cover with water and cook (simmer) 10 to 15 minutes.

Stir in corn, stir in evaporated milk. Heat thoroughly.

Float 2 Tbsp. butter on top and serve.

Serves: Lots

# LONDON CHOP HOUSE - DETROIT, MI WATERCRESS SOUP

1 bunch watercress, stems removed
  (2 cups leaves)
1 cup chopped zucchini
1 cup chopped leeks
1 cup chopped, peeled potatoes
1/2 cup chopped Boston lettuce
1/2 cup snipped parsley (leaves and stems)
1/4 cup sliced green onion
3 teaspoons chicken bouillon granules
2 cups water
1 cup whipping cream
Dairy sour cream
Green onion tops, finely cut
Salt and pepper

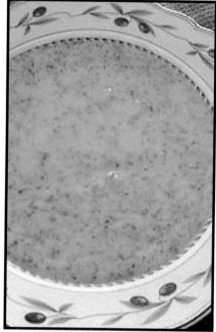

In large saucepan, combine watercress, zucchini, leeks, potatoes, lettuce, parsley, the 1/4 cup onion, and bouillon granules. Add water, simmer covered for 10 to 15 minutes, till potatoes are tender. Pour half at a time into blender container; blend till very fine. Strain; discard vegetables. Season broth to taste with salt and pepper. Add whipping cream; heat through (do not boil).

Combine sour cream, green onion tops, and salt and pepper to taste; spoon atop each serving. Makes 4 servings.

# DEBBIE'S SEAFOOD CHOWDER

*Debbie Balas*

1/2 cup butter
3 cup diced onions
1/2 cup grated carrot (yes, carrot!)
2 tsp. garlic, minced
1/2 cup flour
12 cup water
6 Knorr fish bouillon cubes*
2 lb. haddock
1 lb. cusk or cod
1/2 lb. shrimp
1/2 lb. scallops
2 cup light cream
1/2 cup grated Monterey Jack cheese
2 cup small cubes *cooked* potatoes
Salt and freshly ground pepper

Heat butter in large stockpot. Sauté onions, carrots, and garlic, stirring often, for about 5 minutes. Remove from heat; slowly stir in flour. Return to heat and cook for 2 minutes. Add water slowly and bouillon cubes. Heat until boiling; simmer for 10 minutes. Add fish, shrimp, and scallops; simmer for 10 more minutes. Stir in cream, cheese, and *cooked* cubed potatoes. Simmer until cheese melts. The cheese will melt right in with the chowder. Warm through and serve with salad and crusty loaves of bread. Recipe make 4 quarts.

You can change the combination of seafood to be used as you like.

* If unavailable, use chicken bouillon cubes (must be Knorr).

# FOSTER'S LOBSTER BISQUE

*Abigail Foster - via Janet Pearce Foster*

*The Fosters own two wooden boats: The schooner "One Day" and the 20 foot strip-planked lobster boat "Gilda T." Since Bob has started lobstering, we know this recipe is family tested and approved. It was given to Janet by Bob's daughter, Abigail Foster.*

1 1/2 lb. cooked lobster meat
1 1/2 cup chicken stock
1/4 cup butter
1/4 cup flour
2 1/2 cup milk
2/3 cup cream
Salt
Cayenne pepper

Remove lobster meat from shells. Boil shells and roe with chicken stock for 15 minutes. Strain. Reserve stock. Melt butter; add flour and stock to make a roux; bring to a boil. Meanwhile, chop 1/4 of the lobster meat into small pieces. Add to milk and scald. Reduce heat and simmer. Combine scalded milk with stock. Add remaining meat. Warm cream and add to soup. Season with salt and cayenne pepper. (Freshly ground white pepper may also be used.)

**My opinions may have changed, but not the fact that I am right.**   25

# CANADIAN CHEDDAR CHEESE SOUP

*Yield: 10 servings*

*LeCellier Steakhouse looks like a wine cellar, tucked away near Canada's Victoria Gardens. This creamy soup, with the zing of Tabasco and Worcestershire sauces, is one of Disney's most requested recipes.*

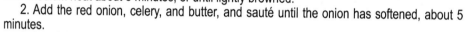

**½ pound bacon, cut into ½ inch pieces**
**4 cups milk**
**1 medium red onion, cut into ¼-inch pieces**
**3 celery ribs, cut into ¼-inch pieces**
**4 tablespoons butter**
**1 cup all-purpose flour**
**1 tablespoon Tabasco sauce**
**Salt, and freshly ground pepper, to taste**
**½ cup warm beer**
**¾ pound grated white cheddar cheese**
**1 tablespoon Worcestershire sauce**
**2 cups chicken stock**
**Chopped scallions or chives, for garnish**

1. In a 4- or 5-quart Dutch oven, cook the bacon, stirring over medium heat about 5 minutes, or until lightly browned.

2. Add the red onion, celery, and butter, and sauté until the onion has softened, about 5 minutes.

3. Add flour and cook, stirring constantly, for about 4 minutes over medium heat. Whisk in the chicken stock and bring to a boil for 1 minute. Reduce heat to a simmer and cook for 15 minutes, stirring occasionally.

4. Add the milk and continue to simmer for 15 minutes. Do not boil after you add the milk.

5. Remove from the heat and stir in the cheese, Tabasco sauce, Worcestershire sauce, salt, and pepper until the cheese is melted and the soup is smooth. Stir in warm beer. If the soup is too thick, add some warm milk.

6. Serve the soup hot, garnished with chopped scallions or chives.

# WILD RICE SOUP

**2 cups cooked wild rice**
**1/2 lb. bacon**
**1 onion**
**2 stalks celery**
**2 cans creamy potato soup**
**1-1/2 qts. whole milk**
**2 cups grated cheese (any kind)**
**1 Tbsp. margarine or butter (heaping)**
**1 Tbsp. cornstarch**

In a kettle fry bacon. Chop onion and celery and add the bacon and cook until veggies are soft. Drain some fat. Add margarine and cornstarch. Stir well. Add remaining ingredients. Stir occasionally. Add salt and pepper to taste.

**If your mother was a better cook, go eat there.**

# The Amazing Cucumber

**1.** Cucumbers contain most of the vitamins you need every day, just one cucumber contains Vitamin B1, Vitamin B2, Vitamin B3, Vitamin B5, Vitamin B6, Folic Acid, Vitamin C, Calcium, Iron, Magnesium, Phosphorus, Potassium and Zinc.

**2.** Feeling tired in the afternoon, put down the caffeinated soda and pick up a cucumber. Cucumbers are a good source of B Vitamins and Carbohydrates that can provide that quick pick-me-up that can last for hours.

**3.** Tired of your bathroom mirror fogging up after a shower? Try rubbing a cucumber slice along the mirror, it will eliminate the fog and provide a soothing, spa-like fragrance.

**4.** Are grubs and slugs ruining your planting beds? Place a few slices in a small pie tin and your garden will be free of pests all season long. The chemicals in the cucumber react with the aluminum to give off a scent undetectable to humans but drive garden pests crazy and make them flee the area.

**5.** Looking for a fast and easy way to remove cellulite before going out or to the pool? Try rubbing a slice or two of cucumbers along your problem area for a few minutes, the phytochemicals in the cucumber cause the collagen in your skin to tighten, firming up the outer layer and reducing the visibility of cellulite. Works great on wrinkles too!!!

**6.** Want to avoid a hangover or terrible headache? Eat a few cucumber slices before going to bed and wake up refreshed and headache free. Cucumbers contain enough sugar, B vitamins and electrolytes to replenish essential nutrients the body lost, keeping everything in equilibrium, avoiding both a hangover and headache!!

**7.** Looking to fight off that afternoon or evening snacking binge? Cucumbers have been used for centuries and often used by European trappers, traders and explores for quick meals to thwart off starvation.

**8.** Have an important meeting or job interview and you realize that you don't have enough time to polish your shoes? Rub a freshly cut cucumber over the shoe, its chemicals will provide a quick and durable shine that not only looks great but also repels water.

**9.** Out of WD 40 and need to fix a squeaky hinge? Take a cucumber slice and rub it along the problematic hinge, and voila, the squeak is gone!

**10.** Stressed out and don't have time for a massage, facial or visit to the spa? Cut up an entire cucumber and place it in a boiling pot of water, the chemicals and nutrients from the cucumber with react with the boiling water and be released in the steam, creating a soothing, relaxing aroma that has been shown the reduce stress in new mothers and college students during final exams.

**11.** Just finished a business lunch and realize you don't have gum or mints? Take a slice of cucumber and press it to the roof of your mouth with your tongue for 30 seconds to eliminate bad breath, the phytochemcials will kill the bacteria in your mouth responsible for causing bad breath.

**12.** Looking for a 'green' way to clean your faucets, sinks or stainless steel? Take a slice of cucumber and rub it on the surface you want to clean, not only will it remove years of tarnish and bring back the shine, but is won't leave streaks and won't harm you fingers or fingernails while you clean.

**13.** Using a pen and made a mistake? Take the outside of the cucumber and slowly use it to erase the pen writing, also works great on crayons and markers that the kids have used to decorate the walls!!

**Worrying works! 90% of the things I worry about never happen.**

# HOLLYWOOD BROWN DERBY COBB SALAD

*The classic Cobb salad is the most-requested entrée at The Hollywood Brown Derby. The story goes that in 1937, owner Bob Cobb and theater magnate Sid Grauman prowled the restaurant's kitchen for a midnight snack resulting in this salad that Grauman ordered again the next day. It became an overnight sensation.*

Yield: 4 to 6 servings

1 cup chopped iceberg lettuce leaves, washed and spun dry
1 cup chopped chicory leaves, washed and spun dry
1 cup tender sprigs watercress, washed and spun dry, plus additional sprigs, for garnish
1 pound poached turkey breast, finely chopped
2 medium-sized ripe tomatoes, peeled, seeded, and finely chopped
1 avocado, peeled, seeded, and finely chopped
½ cup crumbled blue cheese (about 2 ½ ounces)
6 strips bacon, cooked crisp, drained, and crumbled
3 hard-cooked eggs, peeled and finely chopped
2 tablespoons snipped fresh chives
½ cup of French dressing
Radicchio cups, watercress sprigs, for garnish for serving

1. Toss the iceberg lettuce, chicory, and watercress together and arrange in a salad bowl.
2. In straight and separate lines, arrange the turkey, tomatoes, avocado, blue cheese, bacon, and eggs on top of the greens.
3. Sprinkle the chives in two diagonal lines across the salad.
4. To serve, present the salad at the table, toss with the dressing, and place in radicchio cups on chilled plates with watercress sprigs as garnish.

# FRIED GREEN TOMATOES

## Dust:

| | |
|---|---|
| 2 cups all-purpose flour | 1 tsp. salt |
| 1 tsp. black pepper | 1/2 tsp. cayenne pepper |
| 1 tsp. garlic powder | 1 tsp. onion powder |
| Blend together and set aside | |

## Tomatoes:

| | |
|---|---|
| 1 cup flour | 3 whole eggs, beaten |
| 4 cups dust | vegetable oil, for frying |
| 4 large green tomatoes, cut into thick slices | |

Dust tomatoes in plain flour, in eggs, then into dust. Fry at 350° until golden brown. Drain on paper and serve hot.

# LOADED BAKED POTATO SALAD

| | |
|---|---|
| 6 med. baked potatoes | 4 strips bacon, crisp and crumbled |
| 1/4 cup chopped green onions | 1 1/2 tsp. dried chopped chives |
| 1/2 tsp. salt | 1/2 tsp. pepper |
| 1/2 tsp. sugar | 1 cup sour cream |
| 1/4 cup mayonnaise | 4 oz. shredded cheddar cheese |

After potatoes are baked, cut them in half lengthwise; cool. When potatoes have cooled, cut into bite-size pieces; put in large bowl. Add bacon, chives, green onions, and cheese. In a separate bowl mix together sour cream, mayonnaise, salt, pepper, and sugar. Pour the sour cream mixture into the potato mixture and mix thoroughly. Chill in the refrigerator.

**I like work. It fascinates me. I sit and look at it for hours.**

# CREAMED SPINACH

2 pounds fresh spinach, rinsed
 well and stemmed
3 tablespoons unsalted butter
1 bunch scallions, trimmed and minced
8 ounces cream cheese,
 at room temperature
2 tablespoons heavy or
 whipping cream
2 tablespoons fresh lemon juice
Salt and freshly ground
 black pepper to taste
½ teaspoon freshly grated nutmeg

1. Place the spinach leaves in a steamer and cook over simmering water just until wilted, 5 to 10 minutes. Drain well, cool slightly, and chop.

2. Melt the butter in a medium-size heavy skillet over medium heat. Add the scallions, and sauté for 5 minutes. Break the cream cheese into small pieces, add it to the skillet, and stir until melted and smooth. Add the spinach to the skillet, and stir well to combine. Stir in the cream and lemon juice, then season with the salt, pepper, and nutmeg. Cook just until heated through, 5 to 7 minutes. Serve at once. Makes 6 to 8 servings.

# SWEET POTATO CASSEROLE

1.5 lb. sweet potatoes (or yams)
1/2 cup granulated sugar
1/2 cup milk
1 beaten egg
3 Tbsp. butter, cubed
1 tsp. vanilla
------- topping -------
1/2 cup packed brown sugar
1/3 cup all-purpose flour
2 Tbsp. butter
1/2 cup pecan pieces
Pecan halves (optional)

**Directions:** Scrub and peel sweet potatoes. Cut off and discard woody portions and ends. Cut potatoes into cubes. Cook, covered, in a small amount of boiling water for 25-35 minutes or until tender. Drain.

*Carol Laski, Susan Badgerow, Paula Barach, Diane Spinek*
*I met up with 9 of my cousins for a fun weekend in Traverse City, MI. Thanks Charlene for sharing your sweet potato recipe.*

Combine hot potatoes, granulated sugar, milk, egg, the 3 T. butter and vanilla. With a wooden spoon, stir to break up potatoes but not completely mash them. Put mixture into a greased 2-quart square baking dish.

To make topping, combine brown sugar and flour; cut in the 2 T. butter until the mixture resembles course crumbs. Stir in pecan pieces and sprinkle crumb mixture on top of potatoes. Bake uncovered in a 350 degree oven about 25 minutes or until set.

*Garnish with pecan halves, if desired (I do 'cauz I love pecans!).* Makes 8 side-dish servings.

**I always take life with a grain of salt, ...plus a slice of lemon, ...and a shot of tequila.**

# CARAMEL APPLE SALAD
### Submitted by Katy Salutes • Hamburg, MI

**1- 8 oz. frozen whipped topping, thawed**
**1- 8 oz. cans crushed pineapple, drained**
**3 Granny Smith apples**
**4 Snickers candy bars**
**1/2 cup chopped peanuts**

Combine whipped topping and pineapple in bowl.

Peel, core, slice and cube apples.

Cube Snickers bar, chop nuts, and mix all together.

# WATERGATE SALAD
### Brad's Grandma Helen Salutes • Submitted by Katy Salutes

**1 large can crushed pineapple (keep juice)**
**1 small pkg. pistachio pudding**
**8 oz. Cool Whip**
**1 pkg. small marshmallows**
**2 bananas**
**walnuts**

Mix pineapple juice and pistachio pudding mix.

Add crushed pineapple.

Fold in Cool Whip.

Then add:

marshmallows, sliced bananas and walnuts.

# YAM "FRIES"

*Next time the craving for French fries strikes, try this light and spicy takeoff from Joy Pierce, of Rye Beach, New Hampshire*

**2 large unpeeled sweet potatoes (about 2 pounds)**
**1 tablespoon olive oil**
**1 teaspoon ground cumin**
**1 teaspoon ground coriander**
**1/4 teaspoon pepper**
**Vegetable cooking spray**

Scrub potatoes; cut each into this (4- x 1/4- x 1/4-inch) strips. Combine oil and next 3 ingredients in a large bowl; stir well. Add potatoes, and toss well to coat. Arrange in a single layer on a baking sheet coated with cooking spray. Bake at 425° degrees for 25 minutes or until browned, turning potatoes after 15 minutes.

Yield: 4 servings (serving size: 1 cup)

**Never hit a man with glasses. Hit him with a rolling pin.**

# TRADE WINDS SALAD

1/2 of a (1 lb.) package Prince® Elbows, uncooked
1 tablespoon butter or margarine
2 tablespoons packed brown sugar
1 (12 oz.) can luncheon meat, cubed or 1-1/2 to 2 cups cubed fully cooked ham.
1 (13 oz.) can pineapple tidbits, drained, reserving 2 tablespoons liquid

| | |
|---|---|
| 1/2 cup cubed American cheese | 1/4 cup mayonnaise |
| 1/4 cup sour cream | 1/2 teaspoon salt |
| Lettuce (optional) | Red grapes (optional) |

Prepare Prince® Elbows according to package directions; drain. In medium skillet, combine butter and brown sugar; heat until melted. Add luncheon meat and cook until browned and coated with sugar mixture. In medium bowl, combine macaroni, luncheon meat mixture, pineapple and cheese. In small bowl, blend mayonnaise, sour cream, reserved pineapple liquid and salt. Add to macaroni mixture; toss to coat. Serve immediately or cover and chill thoroughly. Toss gently before serving. Serve in lettuce-lined bowl. Top with grapes. Refrigerate leftovers. 6 servings

# ULTIMATE MAC & CHEESE, SOUTHERN STYLE
*Sylvia Waldsmith • 23 in the Morning With Andy & Aaron*

1/2 (16-oz.) pkg. elbow macaroni
salt
4 Tbsp. butter
2 large eggs
1 can evaporated milk, warmed
1/4 tsp. Tabasco, or to taste
ground black pepper
1 tsp. dry mustard dissolved in 1 tsp. water
1 cup shredded Monterey Jack cheese
1 cup cubed Velveeta
1 cup shredded sharp Cheddar

In a heavy bottom pot (such as a Dutch oven), bring 2 quarts of water to boil, add 2 tsp. of salt, and macaroni, cook until tender but not mush. Drain and return to pot, stir in butter to melt. While macaroni is boiling, combine eggs, 1 cup warm evaporated milk, Tabasco, mustard mixture, 1/4 tsp. salt and pepper in a small bowl, over medium-low heat, pour egg mixture and cheese over noodles and stir constantly to melt. Gradually stir in remaining milk, and continue stirring until sauce thickens and mixture is hot and creamy, about 5 minutes. Serve immediately. Will serve 4 as main dish, or 6 to 8 as a side dish.

Note: OK, you're questioning my Velveeta, right? Velveeta adds creaminess..... just try it!!! Process cheese and evaporated milk help keep the sauce from "breaking". Eggs in Mac & Cheese, very Southern!!! Again, they add creaminess.

# CHICKEN SALAD
*Jo Doyle*

| | |
|---|---|
| 3 cup cooked chicken breast | 1/2 cup celery, sliced |
| 1/2 cup green grapes, cut in half | 1 cup pineapple chunks |
| 1 cup pecan halves | Salt to taste |
| DRESSING: | |
| 1 cup mayonnaise | 1 Tbsp. sugar |
| 1/4 cup pineapple juice | |

Cut cooked chicken into bite-size pieces. Combine with rest of salad ingredients. Combine dressing ingredients and pour dressing over salad. Mix well and chill. Serve over lettuce.

**I used to be indecisive when cooking. Now I'm just not sure.**

# ANDOUILLE DIRTY RICE

*Created by Executive Chef John Besh of Restaurant August, New Orleans*
*Prep Time: 14 minutes • Cook Time: 60 minutes*

**2 tablespoons cooking oil**
**1 1/2 tablespoons flour**
**1/2 cup finely minced onion**
**1 cup andouille sausage, removed from casing and chopped in food processor**
**1 rib celery, finely minced**
**1/4 cup finely minced bell pepper**
**1/2 tablespoon minced garlic**
**1 package Zatarain's Dirty Rice Mix**
**1/2 pound chicken or duck livers, finely minced (optional)**
**2 1/4 cups chicken broth**
**1/2 cup chopped green onion**
**1 tablespoon minced parsley**

1. Combine cooking oil and flour in heavy bottomed 6 to 8-quart sauce pot over medium-low heat. Stir with wooden spoon, until color of mixture is similar to dark chocolate, about 20 to 25 minutes.

2. Add onion, continue stirring until soft, about 2 to 3 minutes. Next, add andouille sausage, celery, bell pepper and garlic; stir to combine. Add rice mix and stir occasionally for 5 minutes, to brown mixture and toast rice. If including chicken/duck livers, add livers and stir for an additional 4 minutes.

3. Stir in broth, raise heat to medium and allow mixture to come to a boil. Cover with lid and simmer over low heat for 25 minutes. Before serving, season with minced green onion and parsley. Makes 6 servings.

**When it comes to cooking, you're never too old to learn something stupid.**

# SAVANNAH RED RICE

*The Low Country's penchant for red rice is reflected in the fact that this dish has remained on the menu throughout the decades.*

**2 medium onions, diced**
**Bacon drippings**
**6 to 8 tomatoes, chopped and cooked,**
    **or 1 (16-ounce) can tomatoes**
**½ teaspoon Tabasco sauce**
**4 strips bacon, fried to a crisp and crumbled**
**2 tablespoons grated Parmesan cheese**

**2 medium bell peppers, diced**
**2 cups cooked rice**
**Salt and pepper**
**1 cup tomato sauce or catsup**

    Preheat the oven to 325°. Brown the onions and bell peppers in bacon drippings. In a large mixing bowl, combine the rice, onions, peppers, tomatoes, tomato sauce, Tabasco, and bacon. Season with salt and pepper to taste. Mix well. Pour into a greased casserole dish and sprinkle the cheese on top. Bake for 30 minutes, or until rice is dry enough to separate. Serves 4 to 6.

    NOTE: You may want to add 1 pound of cooked shrimp, sausage, pork or ham.

# EASY FRUIT SALAD

**1 big can fruit cocktail or**
  **2 regular size**
**2 cans mandarin**
  **oranges**
**1 cup coconut**
**1 cup mini**
  **marshmallows**
**8 oz. sour cream**

    Drain cans of fruit, add coconut & marshmallows gently mix fold in sour cream.
    Cover & Chill before serving.

# PEAS 'N RICE

*A staple of the Bahamian diet, simple to make, and with ingredients readily available back home.*

**1 can blackeye or pigeon peas**
**1 1/2 cups rice**
**2 Tbsp. chopped tomatoes**
**1 medium onion, chopped**
**1-6 oz can tomato paste**
**Pepper and salt**
**Thyme**
**2 slices bacon or ham skin from picnic ham, cut small**

In large pan with tight fitting lid, fry bacon or ham skin. Add tomatoes, tomato paste, onion, thyme, salt and black pepper. Steam down. Add peas (drain and retain liquid), stir gently to mix. Add rice and retained liquid plus 1 cup water. Bring to boil, lower heat and cover tightly. Cook until rice is tender and dry – about 20 minutes.

# ESCALLOPED CORN

*by Robin Lindenberg*
*This goes great with any wild game bird or chicken or turkey.*

Mix
**1 pkg. Corn bread mix**
**1 egg**
**½ - cup sour cream**
**½ - cup sugar**
**1 can whole corn**
**1 can creamed corn**

Grease 8x8 baking pan or dish. Pour in mixture. Melt 1 stick butter and pour over mixture. Bake at 350º for 45 minutes to 1 hour. (Until golden brown and set.)

Double recipe for 13x9 pan.

*(Staff note: Robin has made this for us here at the Porky, and we all say, mmmmmmmmmmmm good!)*

# ASIAN SLAW

*Jill Escarmillo*

**1 pre-packaged bag of coleslaw**
**3 chopped green onions**
**1 pkg. Oriental Ramen noodles, toasted**
**Oriental spice pouch from Ramen noodles**
**1/2 cup toasted sunflower seeds**
**1/2 cup toasted almond slivers**
**3/4 cup olive oil**
**6 Tbsp. rice wine vinegar**
**1/2 cup sugar**
**1/2 tsp. ground ginger**
**1/2 tsp. pepper**
**2 tsp. salt**

Toast sunflower seeds, almond slivers and Ramen noodles. Place to the side. Mix dry ingredients together, then slowly add oil and vinegar. Pour over slaw. Top with green onions, toasted sunflower seeds, almond slivers and Ramen noodles. Toss and serve.

**Does this dish rag smell like chloroform to you?**

# Texas Chili Cook-Off

Recently I was honored to be selected as an Outstanding Famous Celebrity in Texas, to be a judge at a chili cook-off because no one else wanted to do it. Also the original person called in sick at the last moment and I happened to be standing there at the judge's table asking directions to the beer wagon when the call came. I was assured by the other two judges that the chili wouldn't be all that spicy and, besides, they told me I could have free beer during the tasting, so I accepted this as being one of those burdens you endure when you're an internet writer and therefore known and adored by all. Here are the scorecards from the event:

## Chili # 1: Mike's Maniac Mobster Monster Chili

**JUDGE ONE:** A little too heavy on tomato. Amusing kick.

**JUDGE TWO:** Nice, smooth tomato flavor. Very mild.

**FRANK:** Holy smokes, what is this stuff? You could remove dried paint from your driveway with it. Took me two beers to put the flames out. Hope that's the worst one. These people are crazy.

## Chili # 2: Arthur's Afterburner Chili

**JUDGE ONE:** Smoky (barbecue?) with a hint of pork. Slight Jalapeno tang.

**JUDGE TWO:** Exciting BBQ flavor, needs more peppers to be taken seriously.

**FRANK:** Keep this out of reach of children! I'm not sure what I am supposed to taste besides pain. I had to wave off two people who wanted to give me the Heimlich maneuver. Shoved my way to the front of the beer line.

## Chili # 3: Fred's Famous Burn Down the Barn Chili

**JUDGE ONE:** Excellent firehouse chili! Great kick. Needs more beans.

**JUDGE TWO:** A beanless chili, a bit salty, good use of red peppers.

**FRANK:** This has got to be a joke. Call the EPA, I've located a uranium spill. My nose feels like I have been sneezing Drano. Everyone knows the routine by now and got out of my way so I could make it to the beer wagon. Barmaid pounded me on the back; now my backbone is in the front part of my chest.

## Chili # 4: Bubba's Black Magic

**JUDGE ONE:** Black bean chili with almost no spice. Disappointing.

**JUDGE TWO:** Hint of lime in the black beans. Good side dish for fish or other mild foods, not much of a chili.

**FRANK:** I felt something scraping across my tongue, but was unable to taste it. Sally, the bar maid, was standing behind me with fresh refills so I wouldn't have to dash over to see her.

## Chili # 5: Linda's Legal Lip Remover

**JUDGE ONE:** Meaty, strong chili. Cayenne peppers freshly ground adding considerable kick. Very impressive.

**JUDGE TWO:** Chili using shredded beef; could use more tomato. Must admit the cayenne peppers make a strong statement.

**FRANK:** My ears are ringing and I can no longer focus my eyes. I belched and four people in front of me needed paramedics. The contestant seemed hurt when I told her that her chili had given me brain damage. Sally saved my tongue by pouring beer directly on it from a pitcher. Sort of irritates me that one of the other judges asked me to stop screaming.

## Chili # 6: Vera's Very Vegetarian Variety

**JUDGE ONE:** Thin yet bold vegetarian variety chili. Good balance of spice and peppers.

**JUDGE TWO:** The best yet. Aggressive use of peppers, onions, and garlic. Superb.

**FRANK:** My intestines are now a straight pipe filled with gaseous flames. No one seems inclined to stand behind me except Sally.

## Chili # 7: Susan's Screaming Sensation Chili

**JUDGE ONE:** A mediocre chili with too much reliance on canned peppers.

**JUDGE TWO:** Ho Hum, tastes as if the chef threw in canned chili peppers at the last moment. I should note that I am worried about Judge Number 3, he appears to be in a bit of distress.

**FRANK:** You could put a hand grenade in my mouth and pull the pin and I wouldn't feel it. I've lost the sight in one eye and the world sounds like it is made of rushing water. My clothes are covered with chili which slid unnoticed out of my mouth at some point. Good, at autopsy, they'll know what killed me. I've decided to stop breathing, it's too painful and I'm not getting any oxygen anyway. If I need air I'll just let it in through the hole in my stomach.

## Chili # 8: Helen's Mount Saint Chili

**JUDGE ONE:** This final entry is a good, balanced chili, neither mild nor hot. Sorry to see that most of it was lost when Judge number 3 fell and pulled the chili pot on top of himself.

**JUDGE TWO:** A perfect ending, this is a nice blend chili, safe for all, not too bold, but spicy enough to declare its existence.

**FRANK:** ------------------

**With sufficient thrust, pigs fly just fine.**

# EASY POT ROAST MARINADE

*Roast (bake) at 325° for about an hour.*
*May be longer depending on size of your roast and pan.*

## Main Ingredients

1 well-trimmed venison roast (2 to 4 lbs or whatever you got handy.) Thaw first if frozen
Plenty of peeled carrots and potatoes rough cut into large chunks
Several stalks of celery, cleaned and cut into chunks
1 or 2 yellow onions, peeled and rough sliced
1 to 3 cups beef or vegetable stock (broth), or plain water

## Marinade Ingredients

Zest of 2 oranges plus juices
Salt & pepper to taste
1/2 cup to 1 cup vegetable oil
1/2 tsp. chopped thyme, fresh or dried
3 fresh garlic cloves, crushed
1 medium onion, rough chopped
1/2 cup red wine vinegar

## Directions

Combine the marinade ingredients in a bowl mixing well. Immerse your thawed roast into the marinade. Store in sealed plastic bag or covered bowl and stash it in the fridge overnight or at least 4 hours. Every so often, reach in and turn the meat around in the marinade to keep it all lubricated evenly.

While you're waiting, get all your veggies prepped and ready to go. Once thawed sear the meat on all sides in a bit of hot oil in a heavy skillet or dutch oven.

Place drained meat in roasting pan, add chopped vegetables and broth. Roast in oven at 325°. Timing will depend on size of roast and how many goodies you included. Plan on about an hour for a 2 pound roast done medium rare.

Tip: To obtain the most juice from the oranges, before cutting press orange down slightly while rolling it across the countertop.

**When hunting for food, shoot first and call whatever you hit the target.**

# LEFTOVER ROAST BEEF-STEW

**Leftover beef, cubed**
**1 small onion, sliced**
**2 stalks celery, sliced**
**2 carrots, sliced**
**1 small green pepper, chopped**
**salt and pepper, to taste**
**thyme & fine herbs to taste**
**dash Tabasco sauce, to taste**
**Worcestershire sauce, to taste**
**1 potato, cubed**
**1 cup gravy, leftover or fresh**

Put all ingredients in a pan, except potato. Cover with water. Bring to a boil. Cover, turn down heat and simmer until tender about ½ hour. (You can freeze at this point.) When ready to serve, heat thoroughly, and add potatoes. Bring to a boil, then turn down heat and simmer until potatoes are done, about 15 minutes. Adjust vegetables to amount of meat. Put in gravy.

**Crust:**
**1 cup flour**      **2 tsp. baking powder**
**¼ tsp. salt**      **¼ cup Crisco shortening**
**a little milk to make a soft dough**

Blend dry ingredients with Crisco. Add milk, knead a little, and roll about ¼" inch thick. Cut in squares. Place on top of meat stew in casserole dish. Bake for 30 minutes at 350°.

• Serves: 4-6 • Prep: 20 min • Cook: 45 min • Easy • Can do ahead • Can Freeze

# CHICKEN ENCHILADAS
*"Double and do ahead for a crowd"*

**2 cups chopped cooked chicken**
**1 - 4-oz. can chopped, mild green chilies**
**1 - 7-oz. jar green chile salsa**
**½ tsp. salt**
**2 cups whipping cream**
**12 corn tortillas**
**salad oil for frying tortillas**
**1 ½ cups Monterey Jack cheese, grated**

Combine chicken, green chilies, and chile salsa and mix well. In medium-sized bowl, mix salt and whipping cream. Heat ½" inch oil in small skillet. Dip each tortilla into the hot oil for 5 seconds; drain on a paper towel. Dip each tortilla into cream, and then fill with chicken mixture. Roll and place in an ungreased baking dish, seam side down. Pour remaining cream over all of the enchiladas and sprinkle with cheese. Bake, uncovered, in a 350° oven for 15-20 minutes.

• Serves: 6 • Prep: 30 min • Cook: 15-20 min • Easy • Can do ahead • Can Freeze

**A bargain is something you don't need at a price you can't resist.**    37

# NO-PEEK BEEF TIPS

1 (1 oz.) package onion soup mix
2 pounds lean stew meat
1 (10¾ oz.) can cream of mushroom soup
1 cup ginger ale

In a greased casserole dish, sprinkle onion soup mix over beef. Spoon mushroom soup over meat: add ginger ale. Do not stir. Bake covered at 350ºF for 2 hours. Don't peek. Serve over rice or noodles.

# BILL CULLEN'S PASTIES

*from Bill Cullen – Caseville*

**PASTRY:**
3½ cups flour, sifted
1 cup vegetable shortening
¼ cup finely chopped suet
Ice water
Salt and pepper to taste

**FILLING:**
1¼ lb. sirloin chopped
4 to 5 potatoes, chopped and peeled
2 onions, chopped
¼ cup rutabaga, chopped

In a large bowl, cut shortening and suet into flour until consistency of course crumbs. Add approximately ½ cup ice water to make soft dough. Divide into 6 portions. Mix all of the filling ingredients. Roll each dough portion on lightly floured board. Place ¾ cup filling on each circle. Salt and pepper to taste. Fold and seal pastry edges over filling and flute. Bake 375º F. for 35 minutes. Reduce oven to 325º F. and bake an additional 15 minutes.

# BEER BATTER

*from Avie Dodt – Sandpoint*

2 cups flour
1 tsp. salt
2 eggs (slightly beaten)
½ cup salad oil
2 tsp. baking powder
1 tsp. garlic salt
2 cups beer

Mix all together, let batter sit for a minute or two. Coat fish, onion rings, or mushrooms with flour and dip in batter then fry.

Some people hear voices.. Some see invisible people.. Others have no imagination whatsoever.

# NEW YORK STEAK WITH PEPPERCORN SAUCE

*from Victor C Leonall – Cheboygan, MI*

4 tsp. cracked black pepper
4 (9 oz.) ¾ inch thick New York strip steaks
2 Tbsp. (1/4 stick) unsalted butter
¼ cup dry white wine
¼ cup Brandy
2 Tbsp. minced shallot
4 garlic cloves, minced
1 cup whipping cream
1 Tbsp. 4-peppercorn blend (or whole black crushed pepper)*
3 Tbsp. sour cream

Rub ½ teaspoonful of black pepper on both sides of each steak. Season steaks with salt. Melt butter in heavy large skillet over high heat. Add steaks and cook to desired doneness, about 3 minutes per side for medium rare. Transfer steaks to plates; tent with foil to keep warm.

Add white wine, brandy, shallot, and garlic to same skillet; bring to a boil, scraping up any browned bits. Boil 1 minute; add cream and peppercorn blend. Boil until reduced to sauce consistency, about 5 minutes. Remove from heat and whisk in sour cream. Spoon sauce over steaks.

*A blend of black, white, pink, and green peppercorns, available in the spice section of many supermarkets.*

# DON'S PINEAPPLE CHICKEN

*from Don Andruizzo - Palatine, IL*

Skinned chicken pieces        Pineapple juice
Pineapple slices              Shake 'n Bake

Preheat oven to 350° F. Dip chicken pieces into pineapple juice, then into Shake 'n Bake. Place into a Pyrex dish and bake for 45 minutes. Remove from oven and add pineapple slices to top of chicken with some pineapple juice. Bake an additional 15 minutes.

**Nostalgia isn't what it used to be.**

# APPLE CHUTNEY PORK TENDERLOIN
*From Rosebank Farms on Seabrook Island*

8 each Pork Tenderloin
2 cups cider vinegar
2 cups sugar
6 green apples, peel 4,
  dice all 3/4"
1/4 cup garlic, minced
1/2 tsp. ground ginger
salt to taste
1 tsp. crushed red pepper
1 1/2 cups raisins
1 Tbsp. dry mustard

**Apple Chutney:**
  Boil the vinegar and sugar for 10 min. Toss in the apples and the rest of the ingredients. Simmer until slightly thick, but the apples still retaining form.

**Pork Tenderloin:**
  Clean off all fat and silver skin. Marinate for 2 hours in 1/4 c. olive oil, & 1/2 tsp. each of garlic, rosemary, mint, salt and pepper or to taste. Grill to desired doneness.

# CHEF DENNIS' FABULOUS STUFFED MEATLOAF
*Like many readers, my mom had a regularly scheduled meatloaf dinner night followed by leftover meatloaf sandwiches for lunch the next day.*

*Now, Mom was a great cook and I learned a lot working beside her and Grandma Stella during my youth. But as fond as my memories are of their individual meat loaves, when my taste buds are shouting "Take me back to the food of my youth, but jazz it up!" I pull out some ground chuck then check out what's on hand that would give it some shimmy and shake style jazz appeal. After all, what's more traditional than meatloaf!*

Today's meatloaf recipe takes advantage of two ingredients you are likely to have on hand: cheese and sliced ham. Keep in mind, like most of my recipes, this one is easy to adjust for portion size and to fit individual tastes, budget, and convenience. If you've got some really picky eaters or have a couple good stuffing ingredients hanging out in the fridge consider stuffing each half of the meatloaf with different but compatible ingredients.

## BASIC MEATLOAF RECIPE
*Yield 6 to 8 servings          Preheat oven to 375° F*

In a large bowl mix all of the following ingredients. Do not over mix or you will break down the fat in the beef and it won't firm up properly when cooking. You're going to want an extra 1/2 to a cup of the ketchup and/or BBQ sauce to brush on top of the meatloaf after it's partially baked.

## MEATLOAF INGREDIENTS
3 lbs. ground beef chuck
1 medium onion small diced
¼ cup ketchup, BBQ sauce or a blend of both

**What kind of rooms have no walls?   Mushrooms.**

1 tablespoon prepared yellow mustard
1 cup bread or cracker crumbs
2 medium to large eggs
2 tablespoons A-1 Sauce (or substitute your favorite brand
1 tablespoon Worcestershire sauce
1 teaspoon granulated of onion (yep, in addition to the onion above)
1 teaspoon granulated garlic
Salt and Pepper to taste (start with approximately 1/2 teaspoon each, diners can add more later plus there's plenty of salt in some of the other ingredients.

## STUFFING INGREDIENTS

4 – 6 ounces sliced cooked ham (deli style works well)
4 ounces shredded Swiss cheese

If you use a box grater to shred the cheese, be sure to use the side with the big holes.

When meatloaf ingredients are fully blended place one half to two thirds of the mixture onto a foil lined sheet pan or pizza pan, something with an edge to keep any grease from the meat from dripping out during baking. Mold meat into a 5" x 12" by 1 inch high loaf, and then form a pocket in the middle to hold the stuffing. Spread the ham and cheese into the pocket evenly. I also try to leave about a half-inch lip when forming the pocket. This way when cut every slice will get some of the stuffing. And, yes, I prefer to use a sheet pan rather than a bread loaf pan. I think it bakes more evenly and it's easier to vary the quantity.

Once stuffing is in place, take the remainder of the meat and pack into place over top of the stuffing making sure to seal the two halves along the sides so that you don't get any leaks. It's not good if your cheese oozes out.

Bake at 375° for 35 to 40 minutes. Remove from the oven and brush or spoon on some ketchup or barbecue sauce on top of the meatloaf. Then return the meatloaf to the oven and continue baking for another 5 to 7 minutes, or until the tomato base topping starts to darken and caramelize. These times may vary depending on your oven. All ovens vary in temperature so you need to know your oven. Bake at least to 155°F for an internal temperature.

The finished meatloaf should be a nice golden brown with a dark red topping. Be careful not to burn the meatloaf or the topping, and of course you want the meatloaf cooked all the way through.

**How do you turn a dish washer into a snow blower? Give her a shovel.**

# TEXAS BEER CHILI

2 lbs. ground beef
2 (8 oz.) cans tomato sauce
1 (16 oz.) can pinto beans
2 Tbsp. chili powder
1 tsp. oregano
1 tsp. salt (to taste)
1 tsp. cayenne pepper of less
1 (16 oz.) can
    peeled tomatoes
1 (12 oz.) can favorite beer
1 small onion, chopped

Cook ground beef in frying pan and drain liquid. Mix beef in large pot with tomato sauce, pinto beans and chopped up can of peeled tomatoes. Add chili powder, oregano, 12 oz. of your favorite beer or 12 oz. of water. Salt lightly to taste and add 1 small onion if desired. Simmer for 10 minutes and then carefully add cayenne pepper. One teaspoon will be quite hot so you may want to try just a little. Stir pepper in slowly and cook another 5 minutes.

# DON LINDENBERG'S SCALLOPED POTATOES
*(secret family recipe)*

Potatoes
Flour
Butter
Milk (1/2 way up the pan)
salt and pepper
Cheese - (optional)

Note: Not exact measurements - it depends on the size of the baking pan how much you use.

Peel potatoes and place in water, (so they don't turn brown).

Slice potatoes and place back in water.

Spray the bottom and sides of shallow baking dish (8 x 8, 9 x 13, etc.)

Layer potatoes, pats of butter, light dusting of flour, salt and pepper and cheese.

Do about 3 layers, or until the pan is full.

Pour milk on, enough so it is about half way up the pan.
Cover and bake at 350° degrees until almost done.
Uncover for the last 15 minutes.

**Save the whales. Collect the whole set.**

# VEGETARIAN TORTILLA CHILI

*Prep Time: 20 Minutes • Start to Finish: 45 Minutes*

1 tablespoon olive oil
1 medium onion, chopped
1 Anaheim or poblano chile,
  seeded, chopped
2 cloves garlic, chopped
2 cans (14.5 oz each) Muir Glen organic
  fire roasted or regular diced tomatoes,
  undrained
1 can (15 oz) pinto beans, drained, rinsed
1 cup water
1 tablespoon chili powder
1/2 teaspoon kosher (coarse) salt
1 medium zucchini, chopped
3 oz. yellow corn tortilla chips
1 medium avocado, pitted, peeled and chopped
1/2 cup shredded Monterey Jack cheese
2 tablespoons chopped fresh cilantro

  1. In 4-quart Dutch oven, heat oil over medium heat. Add onion, chile and garlic; cook 5 to 7 minutes, stirring frequently, until tender.

  2. Stir in tomatoes, beans, water, chili powder and salt. Heat to boiling. Reduce heat to low; cover and simmer 20 minutes, stirring occasionally. Stir in zucchini. Simmer uncovered 5 to 7 minutes longer, stirring occasionally, until zucchini is tender.

  3. To serve, place tortilla chips in individual serving bowls. Spoon chili over tortilla chips. Top with avocado, cheese and cilantro.   6 servings (1 cup each)

# TEXAS-STYLE BEEF CHILI

*Prep Time: 25 Minutes • Start to Finish: 1 Hour 55 Minutes*

1 tablespoon olive oil
2 lb boneless lean beef top round steak, trimmed of fat, cut into 3/4-inch pieces
1 medium onion, chopped
2 cloves garlic, chopped
1 can (14.5 oz) Muir Glen organic diced tomatoes, undrained
1 can (4.5 oz) chopped green chiles, undrained
1 can (14 oz) reduced-sodium beef broth
2 tablespoons chili powder
2 tablespoons yellow cornmeal
1/2 teaspoon kosher (coarse) salt
1/4 teaspoon ground red pepper (cayenne)
Cornbread wedges, if desired
Sliced green onions or chopped fresh cilantro, if desired

  1. In 4-quart Dutch oven, heat oil over medium-high heat. Add half of beef; cook 4 to 6 minutes, stirring frequently, until browned. Remove from pan. Repeat with remaining beef. Return all of the beef to pan. Add chopped onion and garlic; cook 2 to 3 minutes, stirring frequently, until onions are crisp-tender.

  2. Meanwhile, in blender, place tomatoes and green chiles. Cover; blend until smooth.

  3. To beef mixture in pan, add tomato mixture, broth, chili powder, cornmeal, salt and red pepper; stir well. Heat to boiling. Reduce heat to low; cover and simmer 1 hour to 1 hour 30 minutes, stirring occasionally, until beef is tender. Serve over cornbread wedges; sprinkle with green onions or cilantro.   *5 servings (1 cup each)*

**On the other hand, you have different fingers.**          43

## WINDSOR - LOS ANGELES, CA
## TOURNEDOS OF BEEF QUEEN OF SHEBA

4 eggplants slices, peeled (14 inch thick)
All-purpose flour
4 tablespoons butter
1/4 cup chopped shallots
2 tablespoons butter
1/2 cup beef broth
2 tablespoons white wine
2 tablespoons Burgundy wine
8 mushroom caps
16 asparagus tips
Salt
Pepper
4 4-ounce beef tenderloin filets
All-purpose flour
4 ounces prosciutto ham, sliced
1/2 cup Hollandaise Sauce

Dip eggplant slices lightly in flour. In 10-inch skillet cook eggplant in 4 tablespoons butter till browned on both sides, about 5 minutes. Remove and keep warm.

In same skillet, cook shallots in 2 tablespoon butter for 1 to 2 minutes. Stir in beef broth and wines. Add mushroom caps. Cover and cook 4 minutes more.

Cook asparagus in boiling salted water till tender. At same time salt and pepper pieces of tenderloin; dip in flour, pan fry in hot fat to desired doneness, about 2 to 2 1/2 minutes per side for rare.

For each serving, on a plate layer eggplant slices, prosciutto, and beef. Remove mushrooms from sauce; spoon about 1 tablespoon shallot sauce over tournedos. Top each with 2 mushroom caps. Pyramid asparagus on side with Hollandaise. Makes 4 servings.

## PORCUPINE MEATBALLS

3 lbs. ground beef
1 onion, chopped
1 green pepper, chopped
1 cup wild rice
1 large can of tomato juice

Seasonings to taste such as nutmeg, seasoned salt, garlic powder, pepper etc. Mix together with meat, onions, peppers, and wild rice. Then form into 2" inch balls and place into electric skillet and pour tomato juice over the top of the balls. Cover and cook for approximately 1 hour, pouring the excess tomato juice over the meatballs every 15 minutes.

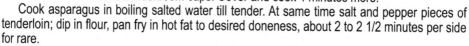

**Support bacteria - they're the only culture some people have.**

# MIDGE'S RIBS

10 lbs. country style ribs
2 med. onions sliced and placed on ribs
   Bake at 450° degrees for 30 minutes

### Sauce:

2 - 28 oz. cans crushed tomatoes
1/2 cup maple syrup
1-1/2 teaspoons cayenne pepper
3/4 cup catsup
3 teaspoons salt
3/4 teaspoon chili powder

8 tablespoons brown sugar
1-1/2 cups apple juice
4 tablespoons Worcestershire Sauce
1 cup white sugar
3 teaspoons dry mustard
1/2 cup vinegar

Simmer while meat browns. Drain all grease off ribs and baste with BBQ sauce every 15 minutes at 350° degrees for 1-1/2 to 2 hours.

# CURRIED CHICKEN

1-2 lbs. chicken (boneless, cooked)
2-4 small onions
1/2 - 1 clove garlic (minced)
1 - 2 Tbsp. soy sauce
1 - 2 tsp. chili powder
1 - 2 tsp. cayenne pepper
1/2 - 1 tsp. turmeric
1/2 - 1 tsp. powdered ginger
1/4 - 1/2 cup vegetable oil
1/2 - 1 cup water
   Simmer for at least 2 hours.

# MR. MIKE'S RECTUM ROASTING CHILI

*Mr. Mike*

2 lb. lean ground beef
1-1/2 chopped Vidalia onion
   (or Spanish)
1 qt. tomatoes
1 chopped bell pepper
1 large can chili beans
1 qt. tomato juice
2 chopped jalapeño peppers
1 chopped habanero pepper
4 oz. chili powder
1 Tbsp. black pepper
2 tsp. salt
1 clove garlic
1 Tbsp. crushed red pepper
1/2 Tbsp. cinnamon

Brown ground beef, sauté onions, peppers and garlic. Combine all ingredients and simmer for approx. 3 to 4 hours. Best served in a bread bowl with an ICE COLD Samuel Adams Boston Lager...

**Love may be blind but marriage is a real eye-opener.**

# CHEF DENNIS' SHEPHERD'S PIE

1 ½ - 2 lbs. Ground Beef
1 to 2 cups brown gravy
1- medium onion small diced
4 – 6 cups shredded cheddar cheese
4 – large potatoes; boiled & mashed
Salt and pepper to taste
2 - tsp. granulated garlic; if using garlic salt you may want to cut back on the other salt.

Optional: Toss a cup of sliced mushrooms into the meat as its cooking.

Preheat oven to 350°F in a conventional oven.

Brown ground beef with the onions on a medium to high heat. Add seasoning once the beef starts to brown. Reduce heat to a simmer until beef has all browned. Remove from heat and drain the excess grease from the pan. Add the gravy to the beef until the mixture is completely moist; not too wet but not too dry. Put beef mixture in a 9 x 12 (or similar size baking pan) spread evenly. Top with the prepared mashed potatoes again spreading evenly. Sprinkle on the cheese, you can use whatever amount you would like. Cover with aluminum foil; bake for 25 to 30 min. Remove foil cook for another 10 to 15 min. until cheese

is golden brown. Remove from oven let it rest for about 15 to 20 min to firm up a little before cutting and serving. - *Photos by Kathy Henderson-Sturtz*

**If at first you don't succeed, destroy all evidence that you tried.**

# HOG HEAVEN CHILI

*Cynthia Zion*

1 lb. Ground Beef
1 large Onion, chopped
1 (10 oz.) can Tomato Paste
1 (16 oz.) can Stewed Tomatoes
1 (16 oz.) can Kidney Beans
1 Tbsp. Chili Powder
2 Tbsp. Sugar
2 Tbsp. White Vinegar
dash of Pepper

1/2 lb. hot Pork Sausage
1 clove Garlic, slivered
1 (13 oz.) can Tomatoes & Chilies
1 (16 oz.) can Pinto Beans
2 (16 oz.) cans Water
1/2 tsp. Cumin
2 tsp. Salt
1 cup Sharp Cheddar Cheese, grated
Sour Cream / Lime Wedges

In heavy skillet cook beef, sausage, onion, and garlic until meat is brown and crumbled, drain grease. Place meat mixture in an 8 quart pot. Add all remaining ingredients except cheese, sour cream & lime wedges. Bring to a boil, stirring often and simmer for 3 hours. Vinegar and Sugar should be added in equal amounts. Add more water as moisture cooks down. Serve with sprinkled grated cheese and a dollop of sour cream. Squeeze lime wedge over chili.

Serves 12 - *Looks complicated but it's not, and it's good!!*

# CHICKEN WAIKIKI

*Joyce Gildner*

2 whole Chicken Legs
2 whole Chicken Breasts
1/2 cup Flour
1/3 cup Salad Oil or Shortening
1 tsp. Salt
1/2 tsp. Pepper
1 (16 oz.) canned Sliced Pineapple
1 cup Sugar
3/4 cup Cider Vinegar
1 Tbsp. Soy Sauce
1/4 tsp. Ginger
1 cube Chicken bouillon
1 large Green Pepper,
(cut crosswise in 1/4 inch circles)
2 Tbsp. Cornstarch

Step 1. Wash chicken. Pat dry with paper towel. Coat chicken with flour.

Step 2. Heat oil in large skillet. Add chicken, a few pieces at a time and brown on all sides. Remove as browned to a shallow roasting pan; arrange piece skin side up. Sprinkle with salt and pepper.

Step 3. Meanwhile, preheat oven to 350° degrees. Make Sauce.

Step 4. Drain pineapple, pouring syrup into a 2-cup measure. Add water to make 1-1/4 cups of liquid.

Step 5. In medium saucepan combine sugar, cornstarch, pineapple syrup, vinegar, soy sauce, ginger and bouillon cube. Bring to boiling, stirring constantly. Boil 2 minutes. Pour over chicken.

Step 6. Bake uncovered, 30 minutes. Add pineapple slices and green peppers. Bake 30 minutes longer. Serves 4

**Experience is something you don't get until just after you need it.**

## POLISH HO-BO DINNER

1 onion
1 1/2 lbs. kielbasa,
   fresh and smoked
6 small carrots
8 small potatoes
4 small ears of corn
1 small head of cabbage
1/2 lb. green and yellow beans

Put kielbasa in kettle, do not cut into pieces; let it circle. Put all the vegetables in kettle and cover with hot water. Cook until the vegetables are tender. When done, drain and serve with mayonnaise and dark bread.

## CHINESE BBQ RIBS

*Quentin E Wells*

2 1/2 to 3 lbs. pork
   spare ribs
4 Tbsp. soy sauce
4 Tbsp. sugar
Hot Sauce:
1 Tbsp. dry mustard
1 Tbsp. vinegar
1 Tbsp. soy sauce
1/2 cup catsup
1/2 tsp. curry powder
pepper to taste

Marinate ribs at least 3 hours in soy sauce and sugar mixture. Bake at 350º for 1 hour and 15 minutes. Baste and turn about every 20 minutes during bake time. Serve with hot sauce while hot. *To use country-style ribs, parboil for 30 minutes first, then follow directions for spareribs.

**Your kitchen creation is done when you get tired of making it.**

# OCTOPUS AND SEAWEED

*Done in 15 minutes or less*
**1 package (3 oz) beef ramen noodles**
**4 hot dogs**
**5 drops food coloring**
**Yellow prepared mustard**

In a saucepan, bring 1-1/2 cups water to a boil. Add the noodles and contents of seasoning packet. Boil for 3 minutes or until noodles are tender.

Meanwhile, add 4 inches of water to a large saucepan; bring to a boil. Cut each hot dog lengthwise into eight strips to within 2 inches of one end. Drop into boiling water; cook until heated through.

Add food coloring to noodles if desired. Drain if necessary. Place noodles on serving plates; top with a hot dog. Add eyes and mouth with dabs of mustard. Yield: 4 servings

**Success always occurs in private and failure in full view.**

# COUNTRY-STYLE STEAK

*This is a favorite family tradition around the holidays, especially for Mrs. Wilkes' great-grandson Ryon. Mrs. Wilkes makes the steak crispy on the outside and tender on the inside. It is best served with white rice.*

**3 pounds cubed steak**
**Worcestershire sauce**
**Pinch of garlic powder**
**Salt and Pepper**
**Flour for dredging**
**¼ cup vegetable oil**
**½ cup minced onion**
**3 tablespoons flour**
**3 1/4 cups water**

Place the steak in a casserole dish and generously sprinkle with Worcestershire sauce. Cover and marinate overnight. Remove from the marinade and sprinkle generously with salt, pepper, and garlic powder. Dip the steak in flour and shake. Heat the oil and quickly fry the steak until brown, but do not cook the inside too much. This is done by cooking both sides on high heat, turning quickly and then reducing heat to low to finish cooking.

Boil ½ cup minced onion in another pot with ¼ cup of the water for about 5 minutes. When finished cooking as many steaks as desired, leave about 3 tablespoons browned crumbs (not burned) and drippings from steak in skillet. Add onion and 3 tablespoons flour. Stir until slightly browned. Slowly pour in the remaining 3 cups hot water as it thickens. Season with salt and pepper to taste. The gravy may be served over rice or steaks. Serves 6 to 8.

# FRYING MIXTURE FOR CHICKEN & FISH

**1 cup flour**
**1 ½ cups milk**
**1 egg, separated and beat yolk and fold in batter.**
Mix and dip your fish or chicken and fry in hot oil.

**The hardness of butter is directly proportional to the softness of the bread.**

Today's Menu

Just Shut UP and Eat It!!

# PASTIE PASTRY

4 cups flour
2 teaspoons salt
1 cup shortening (preferably lard)
Cold water (enough to hold dry ingredients together)

Combine flour and salt. Cut in shortening. Add enough cold water until mixture forms a ball.

Divide into five portions. Pastry can be refrigerated until ready for filling.

## PASTIE FILLING

1 ¼ pounds ground or chopped beef or sirloin steak diced
5 medium potatoes, diced
5 small onions, chopped
¼ cup rutabaga
5 small carrots, chopped
Salt and pepper to taste
5 teaspoons butter or suet

Mix meat, vegetables, salt and pepper and butter or suet together. When combined, it should be enough to fill five pastie crusts. Place mixture in center of pastry square and wrap tightly, sealing crust at ends and side. Bake in 350 degree oven for about 45 minutes of until golden brown.

*Mrs. Laitinen says Finnish pastie enthusiasts never serve the meat pie with gravy. "We prefer butter or ketsup," she says. If you want to freeze pasties for later menus, Mrs. Laitnen says it's best to bake and then freeze rather that freezing before cooking.*

# LEHTO'S PASTIES

*Prep Time: Approximately 60-65 minutes • Serves 4*

*Pasties were introduced to the Upper Peninsula area back in the '70's and '80's when the sturdy Cornish miners first came from England to work in the copper mines. And with them came their wives to make pasties, a one-course dinner the miners could carry in their coat pockets, born of necessity many decades before the invention of the dinner pail. The secret of the popularity of the pastie is that it will remain hot for many hours. Lehto's Pastie Shop can still be found 6 miles west of St. Ignace, Upper Michigan on US 2.*

Makes 4 Pasties

3 cups sifted flour
¼ cup scraped suet
1 ¼ lbs. sirloin steak, diced
¼ cup sliced rutabaga
Salt and pepper

¾ cup shortening and lard mixed
Water as needed
2 medium onions, sliced
¼ cup sliced potatoes

1. Sift flour into mixing bowl; add shortening, lard and suet and cut in until coarse crumbs are formed. 2. Add just enough water to make soft dough, then divide into four parts; roll or pat out into a good-sized circle. 3. Combine meat, potatoes, onions and rutabaga; divide the mixture and place on one side of pastry rounds; sprinkle with salt and pepper and fold remaining pastry over filling; seal edges together. 4. Bake at 375 degrees 45 to 50 minutes, reducing heat during the last 15 minutes to about 350 degrees.

**Two wrongs in a recipe are only the beginning.**

# UNSTUFFED CABBAGE

*Pauline 4-19-86*

1 ½ lb hamburger
1/4 cup water
2 eggs, beaten
3 Tbsp. cooked rice (optional)
3 tsp. minced dry onions - to use in 2 mixes
1 can 28 oz. tomato paste
1 ½ tsp. salt
½ tsp. pepper
1 can 28 oz. tomatoes, chopped
½ cup vinegar
½ tsp. brown sugar
1 med. head chopped cabbage
COMBINE:

Beef, water, beaten eggs, 2 tsp. of the dry onion, pepper & salt. Mix and form into golf ball size balls.

In another bowl mix tomatoes, tomato paste, 1 tsp. dry onion, vinegar and brown sugar and mix. Chop or shred cabbage – place ½ cabbage in casserole on bottom – ½ tomato mixture, ½ meat balls – repeat til all ingredients are used.

Cover with foil and bake at 350° 1 hour then 250° for 3 hours.

# AMISH BAKED CHICKEN

*Norm Webb*

1. Cut up a whole chicken and set aside.

2. Mix 1 Tbsp. of lemon juice or Real Lemon®, 2 Tbsp. of brown sugar and 1 Tbsp. of salt. Mix this in a large glass bowl filled with cold water and add the chicken pieces. (Add enough cold water to completely cover the chicken.)

3. Soak the chicken overnight in the refrigerator.

4. Rinse the chicken pieces in clear cold water and place in a strainer to drain off most of the water.

5. Crush Rice Krispies® with a rolling pin until its fine; this recipe will take about one box of Rice Krispies®.

6. Salt and pepper the chicken pieces and roll them in the Rice Krispies®, make sure all the chicken is covered.

7. Grease a cookie sheet or use Pam® spray and place chicken on the cookie sheet.

8. Melt enough butter or margarine and put only 2 drops and no more than 2 drops on each piece - its very important to do this.

9. Bake in a 350° oven for 1 hour and 20 minutes.

10. Watch it closley and take out of the oven when it is just a little crunchy on the outside, sit back and enjoy. You will think you are eating fried chicken!

*Once you have tried this recipe, let me know what you think.*

*Contact me at: norman_webb45@yahoo.com*

**Change is inevitable except from vending machines.**

# New Standard Operating Procedures for BBQ released today please learn

We are about to enter the BBQ season. Therefore it is important to refresh your memory on the etiquette of this sublime outdoor cooking activity. When a man volunteers to do the BBQ the following chain of events are put into motion:

Routine...

(1)   The woman buys the food.

(2)   The woman makes the salad, prepares the vegetables, and makes dessert.

(3)   The woman prepares the meat for cooking, places it on a tray along with the necessary cooking utensils and sauces, and takes it to the man who is lounging beside the grill - beer in hand.

(4)   The woman remains outside the compulsory three meter exclusion zone where the exuberance of testosterone and other manly bonding activities can take place without the interference of the woman.

Here comes the important part:

**(5)   THE MAN PLACES THE MEAT ON THE GRILL.**

More routine...

(6)   The woman goes inside to organise the plates and cutlery.

(7)   The woman comes out to tell the man that the meat is looking great. He thanks her and asks if she will bring another beer while he flips the meat.

Important again:

**(8)   THE MAN TAKES THE MEAT OFF THE GRILL AND HANDS IT TO THE WOMAN.**

More routine...

(9)   The woman prepares the plates, salad, bread, utensils, napkins, sauces, and brings them to the table.

(10)   After eating, the woman clears the table and does the dishes.

And most important of all:

(11)   Everyone **PRAISES the MAN and THANKS HIM**   for his cooking efforts.

(12)   The man asks the woman how she enjoyed 'her night off',   and, upon seeing her annoyed reaction, concludes that there's just no pleasing some women.

**Plan to be spontaneous - tomorrow.**          53

# A Guys *"ALL WEEK"* Meat Loaf

*by Michael Van Den Branden*

**2 lbs. Ground Beef Chuck**
**2 lbs. Jimmy Dean Pork Sausage – HOT**
**1-1/2 lbs. Mama Russo's Sicilian Hot Cudighi Sausage**
**¼ lb. Butter**
**2 medium Onions**
**3 large Peppers – 1 Green, 1 Red and 1 Yellow (if available)**
**6 oz. Kermit's Key West Lime Shoppe – Cilantro Salsa**
**3 Eggs**
**1 tsp. Celery Seed**
**1 tsp. Nutmeg**
**½ tsp. salt**
**12 oz. A.1. Steak Sauce**
**1 cup Kellogg's All-Bran Original High Fiber cereal**

**To start:** Make sure you have everything you need, or start guessing what you got that will work just as well, maybe. Throw the chunk of butter in a good size frying pan and set the heat on real low to let the butter melt. Don't just stand there and watch it melt, you have a lot of other things to do. Skin the onions and dice up and toss that all into the melting butter. Wash the peppers, core and clean out all the seeds and junk inside. If it is around St. Patrick's Day…use all green peppers…or if your store is like our CO-OP then just be glad they had green peppers 'cause you can bet you won't find red or yellow ones. After you are sure all the seeds are out of them, cut them up into quarter inch pieces…just guess at the size…you don't have to get a tape measure out to check these. The important thing is to remove the seeds, you don't want anybody starting to grow their own pepper inside their body. On an x-ray machine, I would figure they would look like tumors and then some doctor would want to be cutting them out of there. Add the pretty pepper pieces to the onions in the butter and now turn the heat up to medium or so and simmer for about 20 minutes. Get those onions looking translucent, like almost clear and they're done.

While the onions and peppers are doing their thing in the butter, get out a BIG bowl and another large size bowl. Put all your meat in the BIG bowl and then start by whipping up the 3 eggs in the other bowl and then dump in all the other stuff you got left, including the cooked onions and peppers, into that bowl and mix it all up. When you're happy about how you did that, then dump all that stuff in with the meat in the BIG bowl and really get your hands into this and keep squeezing it all through your fingers, over and over again until you are sure you have it all

**"I don't even butter my bread; I consider that cooking." - Katherine Cebrian**

Porcupine Press Upmag
In the oven. This is the very best Sweet Potato recipe!

Ruth's Chris Sweet Potato Casserole Recipe –
Food.com – 278583
www.food.com

This is absolutely divine! Ruth has done it again! Note, the
first time I made this I noticed there was a bit of extra
liquid left over, next time I will adjust the amount of butter
and/or add a bit more potato.

Like · Comment · Share · April 8 at 11:40am · 

👍 Little John, Randy Vile and 4 others like this.

Joe Smith Many years ago you guys published the Man's All-
week Meatloaf recipe. It has become my Easter signature
dish, and the whole family loves it and will be here this
afternoon for Grampa's Traditional Easter MeatLoaf!
April 8 at 2:03pm · Like

Kath Usitalo I want that meatloaf recipe!
April 8 at 2:47pm · Like

Joe Smith @Kath, if we can't get Robin to run it again, I can
send you a copy of a food-stained copy. It's delish!!
April 8 at 3:49pm · Like · 👍 1

Porcupine Press Upmag I will be happy to re run Cap'y
Mike's Meatloaf recipe! It is good, very good!
April 8 at 7:11pm · Like · 👍 1

mixed up as best you can.

Pre-heat the oven to 325° and get out a medium sized roasting pan and your big ball of meat and whatever and put it in the roaster and pat it down tight and then shape the concoction into something that resembles a turkey – but without the legs and the wings. I don't put a top on the roaster because I am like a little kid and keep opening the oven and looking at it baking a lot. Bake for 1 ¾ hours.

Hold it…you're not done yet, while the loaf is baking is the time to clean up all the bowls and tools you used and get the kitchen looking better than before your started. By then the oven will be putting out heavenly smells…don't start eating all the junk food insight and spoil your dinner…instead go for a walk for an hour and build up a big hankering for dinner when you get back.

A special note on some of the super-special stuff that I have thrown into the meat loaf. The purpose of using the Kellogg's All-Bran Original High Fiber cereal is three fold: it sops up a lot of the juices and keeps the loaf moist but still held together, it is the most recommended cereal in the Atkins or South Beach Low-carb diet and it has a very important certificate in the back of the box worth 100 American Airlines miles. The use of the Kermit's Keywest Lime Shoppe – Cilantro Salsa is so I have to go back there every winter…with my air miles…to restock for the next year's meat loaf bakings.

Leftovers are the really great part of this whole operation. You have cooked for about a week. For breakfast; I just fry up a slab with my eggs and whatever, for lunch; I fry up another slab and slap it between two pieces of bread… one side I smear with horseradish sauce and the other with catsup. Excellent with a dark beer, or a light beer in the dark. Cut up some of the loaf and mix in with some potatoes and it makes a good hash. And on, and on, and on, until it is all gone.

**"A friend doesn't go on a diet because you are fat." - Erma Bombeck**

# ITALIAN VENISON SANDWICHES

2 cups water
1 tablespoon dried parsley flakes
1 tablespoon beef bouillon granules
¼ teaspoon garlic powder
1 envelope onion soup mix
1 tablespoon dried basil
½ teaspoon celery salt
¼ teaspoon cayenne pepper
¼ teaspoon pepper
1 boneless venison roast (3 to 4 pounds) cut up into 1-inch
10 to 12 sandwich rolls, split
Green pepper rings, optional

   In a slow cooker, combine the first nine ingredients. Add venison and stir. Cover and cook on low for 8 hours or until meat is tender. Using a slotted spoon, spoon onto rolls. Top with pepper rings if desired.  Yield: 10-12 servings

**"Behind every great man is a woman rolling her eyes." - Jim Carrey**

# HOT ROAST VENISON

*R.L. Rehbein • Colorado Springs, Colorado*

4 lb. venison roast
1 med. whole onion
1 Tbsp. Italian seasoning (dry package)
2 Tbsp. French dressing
dash of oregano
2 cups water

1 stalk of celery
1 Tbsp. vinegar
1 Tbsp. Worcestershire sauce
½ tsp. black pepper
dash of garlic salt

Put all ingredients in a large heavy pot or slow cooker. Cook 5 to 6 hours on top of stove. (Approximately 8 hours in a slow cooker.) Remove onion and celery and add salt to taste.

*Bear meat is the gourmet's delight, especially young animals. It is rich, tender and delicious. Young animals may be cooked in the same manner as beef. Older animals may need marinating. See instructions below for a simple marinade. All fat should be trimmed off before cooking. To avoid dry meat, it should be larded, either by piercing the meat in several places and inserting pork or bacon strips in the opening, or by fastening strips of fat or bacon around the meat when roasting. Bear meat **must be cooked until well done** to prevent trichinosis.*

(Simple marinade, easiest and most economical: take equal parts vinegar and water, and soak the meat overnight or longer, if the meat is from an older animal. For special flavor, you may prefer the marinade below:

1/2 cup wine, sherry, or apple juice
1/4 cup salad oil
strong spices as desired

1/4 cup vinegar
1 grated onion

Soak meat overnight in the combined mixture for young meat, and up to three days for older, tougher meat. However, if young venison and bear meat are properly prepared, the natural flavor should not be tampered with by marinating, until you have tried it without.

# ROAST BEAR

5 lbs. bear roast
1/2 cup vinegar
3 strips bacon
3 Tbsp. margarine
1/4 tsp. pepper

4 cup water
1 Tbsp. salt
1 onion, quartered
1 tsp. salt

Trim and wash meat. Soak for 2 hours in water, vinegar and salt solution. Remove from brine and dry. Place in roaster with bacon on top, and onion around it. Roast for 3 hours at 350º F. Remove bacon. Brush roast with margarine, and sprinkle with salt and pepper. Roast another 15 minutes, basting with margarine meanwhile. Serve hot.

# BEAR STEW

3 lbs. bear meat
1 cup vinegar
1 chopped green pepper
1 tsp. salt
2 cups tomato catsup

1 gallon water
1 medium chopped onion
2 cups chopped celery
1/2 tsp. pepper

Remove all fat from meat, and rinse in cold water. Cut meat into cubes. Mix water and vinegar, and soak meat in the solution for 30 minutes. Drain off liquid and dry the meat. Place all vegetables and seasonings, except catsup, in a deep frying pan with the meat, and cook until well browned. Cover with catsup and simmer for 2 1/2 hours, or until tender.

# VENISON STEAK WITH MUSHROOMS & ONIONS

As in much of Michigan, deer in Huron County where I live, feed primarily on corn. They help themselves to as much as they want with a few side munchies of carrots, sugar beets, beans and nutrient-rich hay. The result is meat with a texture more like that of beef cattle and not as gamey as deer who must scrounge for a living.

Whether I've got pampered venison or a more gamey variety, I still like to marinate it for at least an hour in the same sauce I use for our venison pot roast. Add or substitute your own favorite seasonings if you've got 'em. I always use granulated garlic, granulated onion, a little bit of kosher salt, and my own sweet darling stand-by: the Original Mrs. Dash. You could call her the 'other woman' in my life. Good thing I've got an understanding Better Half that likes Mrs. Dash almost as much as I do. Mrs. Dash and I have been an item since the 1990's. There aren't too many days that I don't use her one way or another.

I rinse my venison before I start to make sure all the hair is removed. Then pat the meat dry before slipping it into the marinade or putting it into hot oil in the frying pan to minimize any grease splattering up. If you use marinade, let some of the sauce drain on a paper towel before adding the meat to the pan, also to reduce splatter. One other tip: To help keep it from sticking, lightly spray both sides of your meat with oil before adding it to the pan.

Adding the bacon to the recipe does several things. It adds a nice smoky flavor, plus moisture and salt. I like my steak with sautéed mushrooms and onions, but they can be omitted. Wild mushrooms not only add a nice flavor but a bit of texture to the visual senses. Woodsy fresh morels are my favorite. My mouth's watering just thinking about serving them up with a good hunk of venison steak. Mmmmmmmm. But, hey, this ain't rocket science; you do it your way.

Doneness is important. I prefer mine medium-rare. So for me I start out with a high to medium-high flame to get the pan hot, then add my oil. By 'oil' I mean any of an assortment of cooking oils such as vegetable, olive, sesame (oriental), peanut, canola, butter-flavored, bacon grease or just a good spraying with a canned coating like Pam. Just be careful because some oils smoke, burn and can burst into flame at much lower heats than others. I usually stick with good olive oil or butter-flavored soy-based cooking oil, same as I use at the restaurant.

Once the oil is hot carefully lay in your steak to let it sear, browning it nicely on one side for

**Smiling increases your face value.**

about 2 to 4 minutes. Now flip it over and turn down the heat to medium and cook the steak another 2 to 4 minutes. The second four minutes should give you a medium done steak. If you want it more well-done, turn the heat to medium-low when you flip the steak. That way the meat won't dry out as much. Regardless of the type of meat your using, searing helps seal in the juices and keeps the meat from tasting like dried out shoe leather.

Add your mushrooms and diced onions when the steak has about one minute left to cook. After the minute or so, remove the steak. Cover it with foil to keep warm and set it aside. Add a bit more oil to the pan if needed and let the mushrooms and onion continue cooking until nicely brown and caramelized. If you removed the bacon earlier, you can add it back now.

Smother the steak with the mushrooms, onions, and bacon and serve with a hefty baked potato and slice of winter squash. Boy, I can smell it now. Actually I can. My plate's waiting on the table and Sweetie is pouring me a beer.

## CHEF DENNIS' VENISON STEAK WITH MUSHROOMS & ONIONS

*Yield: Hey, depends on size of your steaks and appetite!*

3 pieces well-trimmed
  venison steak
4 slices bacon
3 cups or so of mushrooms
1 to 2 cups sliced onion
Venison Pot Roast Marinade

## CHEF DENNIS' VENISON POT ROAST MARINATE

*Yield: Makes about 4 cups.*

2 cups beer
1/2 cup red or white wine
1/4 cup brown sugar
1/4 cup balsamic vinegar
1/2 cup vegetable oil
1/2 fresh lemon, squeezed
  (about 1 tablespoon juice)
1 tsp. Worcestershire sauce
1/4 tsp. dry mustard
1/2 cup ketchup
3 garlic cloves, crushed
1/2 white onion, sliced

Directions: Combine ingredients well in deep bowl. Add meat. Cover and chill at least 1 hour. Longer is better, even overnight especially if your venison is more gamey. You can easily alter this recipe to suit your own taste buds and what you have on hand.

# RECIPE FOR HAPPINESS

One half cup of friendship,
One cup of thoughtfulness
Creamed together with a pinch of
    powdered tenderness.
Very lightly beaten,
In a bowl of loyalty;
With one cup of faith, and one of hope,
Add one of charity.
Be sure to add a spoonful each of
Gaity that sings,
And also the ability to laugh at little
    things.
Moisten with sudden tears of heartfelt
    sympathy.
Bake in a good natured pan.
Serve repeatedly........
Try this recipe..... It's very good!!

**Never iron a 4-leaf clover, you don't want to press your luck.**

# LOWCOUNTRY BOIL

*Seewee Restaurant*

3 lbs. small white potatoes
  salt and pepper to taste
Old Bay seasoning to taste
5 lbs. shrimp, shells on
3 dozen small clams, in shell
1 whole sliced lemon
3 garlic cloves
3 lbs. Hillshire Sausage, cut in 1 inch
slices
5 lb. bag corn-on-the-cob,
  fresh or frozen

Put potatoes and seasoning in pot with enough water to cover; simmer until almost done. Add sausage and corn; cook until done. Add clams and shrimp; cook until pink. Serve hot.

# DOOR COUNTY FISH BOIL

*It's traditionally served with garden fresh coleslaw and homemade breads.*

2 Gallons Water
½ Cup Salt
18 Small Red Potatoes
  (If large, cut in half or quarters)
6 Whitefish Fillets (About 6
  Ounces Each) or other mild,
  White Fish
8 Tablespoons Butter, Melted
2 Lemons, Cut Into Wedges

1. Bring the water to a rolling boil. Add the salt and potatoes.

2. Cook for 10 minutes or until partially done.

3. Add the fillets and cook for 8 to 10 minutes, or until the fish is firm and begins to flake. Skim any film that forms on top of the water.

4. Remove the potatoes and fish from the water. Place on a platter and serve with the lemon wedges and individual dishes of butter.

YIELD: 6 servings • PREPARATION TIME: 5–10 minutes • COOKING TIME: About 25 minutes (not including boiling the water)

**The problem with the younger generation is ~ I'm not in it.**

# CHARLEYS' CRAB - TROY, MI
# BAKED STUFFED LOBSTER LARRY

1 cup fresh mushrooms, sliced
1/4 cup chopped onion
2 tablespoons butter
1 tablespoon all-purpose flour
1/4 teaspoon salt
dash pepper
1/3 cup milk
1 slightly beaten egg yolk
1/4 cup fine dry bread crumbs
6 ounces frozen crab meat or
  1- 7-ounce can crab meat, drained,
  flaked and cartilage removed
2 live lobsters
  (about 1 1/2 pounds each)
4 tablespoons butter, melted
Lemon wedges

In saucepan, cook mushrooms and onion in the 2 tablespoons butter; stir in flour, salt, and pepper. Add milk all at once; cook and stir till thickened and bubbly. Stir about half the hot mixture into beaten egg yolk; return all to saucepan. Cook and stir one minute more. Add bread crumbs, then carefully fold in crab meat. Set aside.

Plunge live lobsters into enough boiling salted water to cover. Return to boiling; reduce heat and simmer 10 minutes. Remove at once. Place on back. With sharp knife, cut in half lengthwise. Remove black vein that runs to tip of tail. Discard all organs in body section near head except red coral roe (females only) and brownish-green liver. Crack claws.

Spoon half of the stuffing mixture into body cavity of each lobster. Brush both lobsters with melted butter. Place in shallow baking pan. Bake, uncovered, in 475° oven for 10 to 12 minutes or till stuffing is heated through. Serve with lemon wedges and any remaining melted butter. Makes 2 servings.

# JOE'S STONE CRAB RESTAURANT - MIAMI
# BEACH, FL • SHRIMP CREOLE

16 ounces fresh or frozen shrimp, thawed,
  peeled, and deveined
1/4 cup chopped celery
1/4 cup chopped onion
2 tablespoons finely chopped salt pork
1 16-ounce can whole tomatoes, cut up
1/4 cup chili sauce
2 teaspoons sugar
1/2 teaspoon dried thyme
1/2 teaspoon beef flavored gravy base
1 clove garlic, minced
Salt and pepper
hot cooked rice

Cook shrimp in boiling salted water 1 to 3 minutes or till done. Drain and set aside. In saucepan, cook celery, onion, and salt pork till celery is tender, about 5 minutes. Add tomatoes, chili sauce, sugar, thyme, gravy base, and garlic. Season to taste with salt and pepper. Cover and simmer 30 minutes. Add shrimp; heat through. Serve with rice. Makes 4 servings.

**A man who drives like hell is bound to get there.**

# BEER-BRAISED SHRIMP

Makes 6 servings • *Serve with an American-Style Premium Lager*

**1/4 cup extra-light olive oil**
**10 garlic cloves, very coarsely chopped**
**1-1/2 pounds (about 36) large shrimp, peeled and deveined**
**1/2 teaspoon cayenne pepper**
**Kosher salt and freshly ground pepper**
**1 bottle (12 ounces) Budweiser**
**1/2 cup fresh lime juice**

Step 1: In a large heavy skillet over high heat, heat the olive oil and garlic until the garlic starts to caramelize, 1 to 2 minutes. Add the shrimp and season with the cayenne and the salt and black pepper to taste.

Step 2: Pour in half of the beer and cook for 5 minutes. Turn the shrimp and add the lime juice and the remaining beer. Cook until the shrimp are firm and the flesh is white throughout. Serve immediately.

# COCONUT SHRIMP WITH ORANGE MUSTARD SAUCE

Prep Time: 15 minutes
**Coconut Shrimp:**

**1 lb. medium size shrimp**
**1/2 cup flour**
**1/2 tsp. salt**
**dash paprika**
**pepper to taste**
**5/8 cup beer**
**1 cup shredded coconut**
**oil for frying**

**Orange Mustard Sauce:**

**2 Tbsp. orange marmalade**
**2 tsp. Dijon style mustard**
**2 Tbsp. orange juice**

1. Clean and de-vein shrimp leaving tails attached. Drain on paper towels.

2. In medium size bowl, combine flour, salt, pepper and paprika. Gradually stir in beer, mix until well blended. Place shrimp in beer batter.

3. Heat 1 inch oil in heavy large saucepan. One by one, remove shrimp from beer batter, allowing excess batter to drip off, and dredge in shredded coconut. Fry in hot oil until coconut begins to brown. Remove with slotted spoon, drain on paper towels.

4. Combine orange marmalade, mustard and orange juice. Serve on the side as a dipping sauce. Makes 20 to 24 appetizers.

**If a parsley farmer is sued, will they garnish his wages?**

# PORT AUSTIN'S BEER BATTER PERCH

**1 cup flour**
**1 egg**
**2 Tbsp. minced onion**
**1-½ tsp. baking powder**
**1 tsp. prepared mustard**
**1 can of beer (of your choosing)**

Mix all, using beer until consistency of batter is obtained. Dip fresh (or defrosted) fillets in batter, deep fry in light oil until golden brown.

# PAN FRIED WHITE LAKE PERCH FILLET

1. In small bowl beat 1 egg and 3/4 cup of cold water using a fork or wire whisk.
2. Using paper towel, pat dry all of the white lake perch, fillets.
3. Dip fillets in egg mixture and roll them in a mixture of 1 part dry Bisquick to one part corn meal.
4. Set plate or breaded fillets in freezer to chill 10 minutes. When chilled, fillets hit hot oil & the outside crisps and seals out the oil.
5. Heat your frying pan up first and then add your oil as this helps prevent sticking during cooking.
6. To test your pan and oil for readiness hold you hand about 6 inches above oil. When you can feel the heat coming off, then it is ready for cooking. (Do not let oil get so hot that it smokes as this will give fish a bad flavor and aroma). (The ideal frying temperature would be just shy of the oil smoking).
7. Take fillets out of freezer and place a single layer into hot oil.
8. Fry each side of fillets until golden brown.

**When you get older, going out is good, but coming home is better.**

Carrots, Eggs, or Coffee.

"Which are you?" she asked her granddaughter.

## Carrots, Eggs, or Coffee: "Which are you?" she asked her granddaughter.

A young woman went to her grandmother and told her about her life and how things were so hard for her. She did not know how she was going to make it and wanted to give up. She was tired of fighting and struggling. It seemed as one problem was solved a new one arose.

Her grandmother took her to the kitchen. She filled three pots with water. In the first, she placed carrots, in the second she placed eggs and the last she placed ground coffee beans. She let them sit and boil without saying a word.

In about twenty minutes she turned off the burners. She fished the carrots out and placed them in a bowl. She pulled the eggs out and placed them in a bowl. Then she ladled the coffee out and placed it in a bowl. Turning to her granddaughter, she asked, "Tell me what do you see?"

"Carrots, eggs, and coffee," she replied.

She brought her closer and asked her to feel the carrots. She did and noted that they got soft. She then asked her to take an egg and break it.

After pulling off the shell, she observed the hard-boiled egg.

Finally, she asked her to sip the coffee. The granddaughter smiled, as she tasted its rich aroma. The granddaughter then asked. "What's the point, grandmother?"

Her grandmother explained that each of these objects had faced the same adversity--boiling water--but each reacted differently.

The carrot went in strong, hard and unrelenting. However after being subjected to the boiling water, it softened and became weak. The egg had been fragile. Its thin outer shell had protected its liquid interior. But, after sitting through the boiling water, its inside became hardened.

The ground coffee beans were unique, however. After they were in the boiling water they had changed the water.

"Which are you?" she asked her granddaughter.

"When adversity knocks on your door, how do you respond? Are you a carrot, an egg, or a coffee bean?"

Think of this: Which am I?

Am I the carrot that seems strong, but with pain and adversity, do I wilt and become soft and lose my strength?

Am I the egg that starts with a malleable heart, but changes with the heat? Did I have a fluid spirit, but after a death, a breakup, a financial hardship or some other trial, have I become hardened and stiff?

Does my shell look the same, but on the inside am I bitter and tough with a stiff spirit and a hardened heart?

Or am I like the coffee bean? The bean actually changes the hot water, the very circumstance that brings the pain. When the water gets hot, it releases the fragrance and flavor. If you are like the bean, when things are at their worst, you get better and change the situation around you.

When the hours are the darkest and trials are their greatest do you elevate to another level? - *AUTHOR UNKNOWN*

**Jokes about German sausage are the wurst.**

# HARVEST APPLE PIE

*A staple of The White Owl Bistro's dessert menu. Recipe courtesy of Debbie Proulx -Laura Dubois' mother*

### Crust:

1/4 cup butter
1/2 cup sugar
1/2 cup flour

Mix together and pat firmly into large pie plate, making sure to press crumb mixture up the sides.

### Filling:

2 pkgs. cream cheese
1/2 cup sugar
2 large eggs
1/2 tsp. vanilla

Cream together and pour into crust.

### Topping:

8 apples
1/3 cup of sugar
1/2 tsp. cinnamon
1/3 cup slivered almonds

Peel, core and slice apples thinly. Arrange apples in a pinwheel on top of cream cheese. Sprinkle with sugar, cinnamon and almonds. Bake in a preheated 350 degree oven for 30-40 minutes or until slightly firm in the middle.

## Best Ever Sweet Potato Pie

1 cup whole milk, scalded
1 cup evaporated milk
1 cup cooked, mashed sweet potatoes
1 tsp. pure vanilla
¾ cup white sugar
¾ cup brown sugar
3 Tbsp. flour
½ tsp. nutmeg
½ tsp. cinnamon
½ tsp. salt
3 eggs, separated
2 (9-inch) unbaked pie crusts

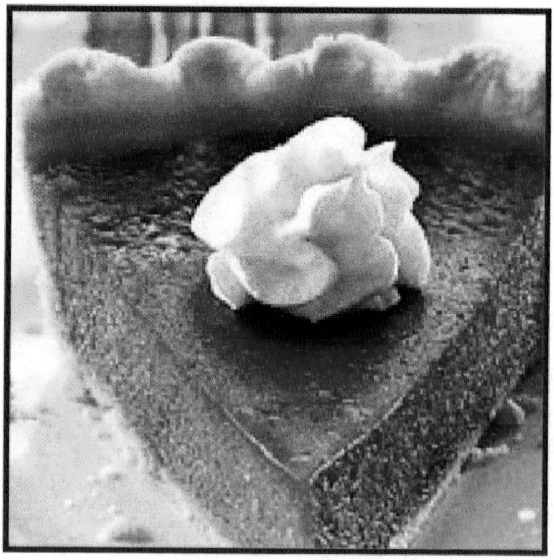

Scald whole milk. Mix together both milks, sweet potatoes, sugars, flour, spices, and salt. Add egg yolks. Whip egg whites until stiff and fold in last. Pour into pie crusts. Bake at 400ºF for 10 minutes, then 350ºF for 45 minutes. Makes 2 pies.

Variation: For crumb topping, mix 1-cup flour, 1-cup brown sugar, 1-cup oatmeal, and 1 stick softened butter. Add to tops of pies before baking.

**SOSUMI - New sushi bar that caters to lawyers.**

**1 1/4 cup solid shortening (I prefer Crisco)**
**3 cup sifted flour (plus a bit extra for rolling)**
**1 tsp. salt**
**1 egg**
**5 Tbsp. water**
**1 Tbsp. vinegar**

Cut shortening into flour and salt. Combine egg, water and vinegar. Pour this liquid mixture all at once into flour mixture. Blend with a fork. Roll out on lightly floured surface. Makes 2 (8" or 9") double crust pie shells or 4 large pasties. This may be doubled. For flaky crust don't overwork dough. And it never fails!

**3 large eggs, slightly beaten**
**¼ teaspoon salt**
**½ teaspoon vanilla**
**¼ cup brown sugar**
**1 cup light corn syrup**
**1 cup raw Georgia peanuts**
**1–9-inch deep – dish pie shell, unbaked**
**whipping cream, whipped and sweetened to taste**

Combing eggs, salt, vanilla, sugar, corn syrup and peanuts. Pour into pie shell. Bake at 450° for 10 minutes, reduce heat to 350° and bake 35 minutes. Chill before serving.

Garnish with whipped cream.

**_Crust:_**
**2 ¼ cups graham cracker crumbs**
**2 tablespoons sugar**

**½ cup butter, melted**
**½ teaspoon ground cinnamon**

**_Filling:_**
**1 envelope unflavored gelatin**
**½ cup cold water**
**5 egg yolks**
**1 cup sugar**
**1/3 cup dark rum (or to taste)**
**1 ½ cups whipping cream, whipped**
**unsweetened chocolate, grated**

For crust, combine all ingredients and press into a 9-in deep-dish pie pan. Chill. For filling, soften gelatin in water. Place over low heat. Bring almost to a boil, stirring to dissolve gelatin. Beat egg yolks and sugar until very light. Stir gelatin into egg mixture. Cool. Gradually add rum, beating constantly. Fold whipped cream into egg mixture. Cool until mixture begins to set, then spoon into crust. Chill until firm. Top with grated chocolate.

_Note: After adding the 1/3 cup of rum-you may finish the bottle during cooking time._

**Of all the things you wear, your expression is most important.**

# SOUTHERN PEANUT PIE

3 eggs
1 & ½ cups dark corn syrup
¼ tsp. salt
1 & ½ cups chopped roasted peanuts

½ cup sugar
¼ cup butter, melted
¼ tsp. vanilla
9 inch unbaked pie shell

Beat eggs until foamy. Add sugar, syrup, butter, salt and vanilla. Continue to beat until thoroughly blended. Stir in peanuts. Pour into unbaked pie shell. Bake in a preheated 375° F oven for 45 minutes. Delicious served warm or cold. May be garnished with whipped cream or ice cream.

# OPEN FACE PIE CRUST

*Makes 1 open face crust*

## DOUGH

1 ¼ cups flour
½ tsp. of salt
Milk to moisten (approx. 5 Tablespoons)

4 Tablespoons of Spry or lard

# UNCLE ROY'S STRAWBERRY PIE FILLING

1 pint water (boil)
1 heaping Tbsp. cornstarch, mix well with the boiling water
1 ½ cups sugar
A few drops of red food coloring
Mix all the above and add to 4 cups cut strawberries. Mix this well, pour into pie crust and bake at 420 degrees oven 10 minutes then turn temperature down to 350° and bake for 35 minutes or until it bubbles in the center! Cool pie and cover with whip cream.

# STRAWBERRY PIE

1-9 inch double crust pie shell
Combine below ingredients with 4 cups cut fresh strawberries.

1 cup sugar        4 Tbsp. cornstarch        ½ tsp. salt

Sprinkle over berries. Pour into the pie crust shell and bake at 420 degree oven 10 minutes then turn temperature down to 350 and bake for 35 minutes or until it bubbles in the center! Oven temps. may vary.

# BLUEBERRY PIE

1-9 inch pie crust shells
1 Tbsp. butter to each pie
1 ¼ cups flour
½ tsp. salt

A sprinkle of lemon juice
1 pie crust
4 heaping Tbsp. lard
Milk to moisten (about 5 Tbls.)

Mix sugar and a little milk and brush on crust.

Mix all the rest with 4 cups berries and pour into the pie crust shell - bake at 420 degree oven 10 minutes then turn temperature down to 350 and bake for 35 minutes or until it bubbles in the center!

**I try to loose weight but it keeps finding me.**

# PEANUT BUTTER PIE

*Doris 1990*

**2 graham cracker crusts
(to pour mixture below into)
1-8 oz. pkg. cream cheese
3 cups Powdered sugar
24 oz. Cool Whip
1 ½ tsp. vanilla
1-8 oz. jar chunky
peanut butter**

Mix with beater and pour into graham cracker crust and put in freezer til cold.

# RHUBARB CUSTARD PIE

*By Gabriel*

1. 1 cup sugar
2. 3 Tablespoon flour
3. 1 teaspoon vanilla
1 -9 inch pie pan

4. 3 egg yokes, beaten
5. 1 cup sweet cream
  2 cups rhubarb

Mix first 5 ingredients then add rhubarb. Pour into pastry lined pan.
Bake for 45 minutes at 375 degrees. Add meringue.

## Meringue

Beat 3 egg whites and ¾ tsp cream of tartar until foamy (beat tartar on high speed).

Gradually beat in 1/3 cup of sugar continue beating until stiff peaks form.

Spread meringue evenly over hot pie sealing to edge of crust.

Bake at 350 degrees for 15-20 min. until golden brown.

**Everyone has a photographic memory. Some don't have film.**

# ELVIS PEANUT BUTTER GOOEY BUTTER CAKES

*Gooey butter cakes are one of my specialties, and they're one of the most popular items on The Lady & Sons menu. I can't tell you how many varieties of gooey butter cakes we've served over the years! This one was sent to us by Brian Proffitt of Lexington, Kentucky. It would be pretty good with a chocolate crust, too.*

## Cake Layer

One 18.25-oz. package yellow cake mix               1 egg
1/2 cup (1 stick) butter, melted

## Filling

One 8-oz. package cream cheese, softened            3 eggs
1 teaspoon vanilla extract
1/2 cup creamy peanut butter
1 ripe banana, mashed with a fork or potato masher
1/2 cup (1 stick) butter                    One 1-lb. box confectioners' sugar

## Garnish

1 cup whipping cream, whipped with 1 tablespoon confectioners' sugar
Mint leaves

1. Preheat the oven to 350ºF. Spray a 13 by 9-inch baking pan with vegetable oil cooking spray.

2. In a large mixing bowl, stir together the cake mix, egg, and butter with a fork, mixing well. Pat lightly into the prepared pan.

3. To prepare the filling, in the same large mixing bowl, beat the cream cheese, eggs, and vanilla. Add the peanut butter, banana, and butter and beat well. Stir in the confectioners' sugar with a spatula, then beat until the mixture is smooth, about 2 minutes. Pour the batter over the cake mixture.

4. Bake for 45 to 50 minutes. You want the center to still be a little loose, so do not overbake. Allow to cool about 15 minutes before slicing.

5. Top each warm cake slice with a dollop of whipped cream and a mint leaf. Makes 16 squares.

# TEXAS SHEET CAKE

*Kera Williams*

**Part 1 -** **1-cup boiling water**
2 sticks oleo or butter
4 Tbsp. cocoa
Stir together
**Part 2 -** Cream together:
2 cups sugar
2 eggs
1 carton sour cream (small)
**Part 3 - Pour hot mixture into creamed ingredients, then add dry ingredients below:**
1 tsp. baking soda                    2 cups flour
½ tsp. salt
Mix will be runny. Grease and flour a jelly roll pan. Bake at 375º for about 20 minute. Frost while cake is hot.
**Part 4 - Frosting**
2 ½ cup powdered sugar           1 stick oleo or butter
4 Tbsp. cocoa                    6 Tbsp. milk (Please Note: I used Chocolate Milk)

**When the chips are down, the buffalo is empty.**

# DRESS UP YOUR CAKE bake as directed

*Submitted by Joann Schmidt - Chesaning, MI*

1. 1 box dark chocolate, 4 eggs, 1 can cherry pie filling.
2. 1 box white, 1 can cherry pie filling, 1 cup chocolate chips, 4 eggs.
3. 1 box spice, 1 can apple pie filling, 4 eggs.
4. 1 box coconut, 4 eggs, 1 can cherry pie filling, 1/2 c. coconut.

*These are separate recipes you can use your imagination on what cake mix to use.*

# FRESH PEACH CAKE

2 cups flour, divided
1 tsp. baking soda
1 tsp. salt
1 tsp. cinnamon
3 eggs well beaten
1 3/4 cups sugar
1 cup vegetable oil
2 cups sliced fresh peaches
1/2 cup chopped pecans
Whipped cream, if desired

In medium bowl, combine 1 1/2 cups of the flour, baking soda, salt and cinnamon; set aside. In large bowl, combine eggs, sugar and oil; beat until smooth. Add flour mixture and beat at low speed just until blended and thick batter is formed. Dredge peaches and pecans in remaining 1/2 cup flour and stir into batter. Spoon batter into greased and floured 13x9-inch baking pan. Bake at 375° degrees, 40 to 50 minutes or until cake starts pulling away from sides of pan and tests done. Do not over bake. Cool on wire rack completely before cutting into squares. Serve with whipped cream, if desired. Makes about 12 servings.

# MANDARIN ORANGE CAKE

*Submitted by: Mozelle White*

1 box butter cake mix (Duncan Hines)
3/4 cup cooking oil
4 eggs

Mix above ingredients in large mixing bowl. Add 1 - 11 oz. can of Mandarin Oranges, juice and all. Mix by hand to prevent mashing the orange sections. Pour into 3 layer, greased and floured cake pans. Bake at 350° degrees for 18 - 20 minutes or till done. Let cakes completely cool.

Fill with frosting.

**Frosting:**

1 can (20- oz.) crushed pineapple
1 small pkg. instant vanilla pudding mix
1 (9 oz.) carton Cool Whip.

Mix all together and frost cake.

**Amazing! You hang something in your closet and it shrinks two sizes.** 71

# BANANA UPSIDE DOWN CAKE

1 stick unsalted butter
1/3 cup orange marmalade or strained apricot preserves
3 cups thinly sliced banana (about 3 bananas)

| | |
|---|---|
| 1/2 cup sugar | 1 egg |
| 1 tsp. vanilla | 3/4 tsp. cinnamon |
| 1/2 tsp. nutmeg | 1/2 tsp. allspice |
| 1 1/3 cups flour | 1/2 cup milk |
| 2 tsp. double acting baking powder | 1/2 tsp. salt |

whipped cream or ice cream

1. Butter, or spray with non-stick cooking spray, a 9 inch cake pan. Spread surface of bottom of pan with orange marmalade or apricot preserves. Arrange banana slices, overlapping, in circles over jam.

2. In large bowl, cream butter. Add sugar, in small amounts, beating, and beat mixture until light and fluffy. Beat in egg, vanilla, cinnamon, nutmeg, and allspice.

3. In another bowl, sift together flour, baking powder, and salt. Stir mixture into butter mixture, 1/2 cup at a time, alternately with milk. Stir batter until just combined.

4. Pour batter over banana slices, smooth top, and bake cake on baking sheet in middle of preheated 350° degree oven 1 hour. Let cake cool in pan on rack 30 minutes. Run thin knife around inside of pan, invert cake plate over pan, and invert cake onto plate. Serve cake with fresh whipped cream or ice cream as desired.

# CHOCOLATE POTATO CAKE

*Shirley Stillwagon  Sister "T"*

| | |
|---|---|
| 3/4 cup Butter (margarine) | 1 1/2 cup Sugar |
| 4 Eggs (separated) | 1 cup Mashed Potatoes Hot |
| 1 1/2 cup Flour | (no butter, milk or seasoning) |
| 2 tsp. Baking Powder | 1 tsp. Cinnamon |
| 1/2 tsp. Salt | 1/2 cup Cocoa |
| 1/4 tsp. Ground Cloves | |
| 1/2 tsp. Ground Nutmeg | |
| 1 tsp. Vanilla | |
| 1 cup Milk | |
| 1 cup Chopped Nuts (optional) | |

Mix butter and 1 cup of sugar. Add egg yolks, beat in warm potatoes. Mix thoroughly. In a separate bowl combine all dry ingredients and spices. Add to the creamy mixture, alternating with milk. Beat until smooth. Stir in vanilla (nuts optional). In a small bowl beat egg whites with an electric mixer until foamy. Add 1/2 cup of sugar and beat until stiff peaks form. Fold into batter. Place in a 9 x 13 inch greased and floured baking dish. Bake at 350° degrees until done (springs back when touched or toothpick placed in center comes out clean). Cool. Frost with Fluffy Frosting.

## Fluffy Frosting:

| | |
|---|---|
| 2 Egg Whites | 1 1/2 cup Sugar |
| 1/3 cup Water | 2 tsp. Light Corn Syrup |
| 1/8 tsp. Salt | 1 tsp. Vanilla |

Combine egg whites, sugar, water, light corn syrup, and salt in the top of a double boiler, beat for 1 minute. Place over boiling water, beat constantly for 5 to 7 minutes, scraping bottom and sides of pan occasionally. Remove from heat, add vanilla, beat for 1 minute. Frost the cake.
- Shown with powdered sugar.

**Four words a wife wants to hear: Honey - I'll fix it.**

# CHOCOLATE MAYONNAISE CAKE

*Sylvia Novak*

**2 cup flour, unsifted**
**1 cup sugar**
**1/2 cup unsweetened cocoa**
**1 1/2 tsp. baking powder**
**1 tsp. baking soda**
**1 cup mayonnaise**
**1 cup water**
**1 tsp. vanilla**

Grease a 9x9x2" pan; line bottom with waxed paper. Grease and flour wax paper. Sift flour. Mix sugar, cocoa, powder and soda with flour. Stir in mayonnaise. Gradually stir in water and vanilla until smooth. Pour into prepared pan. Bake at 350° for 40 to 45 minutes until done. Cool completely before removing from pan. Remove waxed paper and frost as desired. Butter cream frosting is excellent.

*This is a very old recipe. You will notice it has no eggs. It is very good.*
*(Note from Robin: I doubled this and it made 36 cupcakes)*

# RHUBARB CAKE

*Teena Miske*

**2 cup flour**
**1 cup sour cream**
**1 beaten egg**
**1 tsp. baking soda**
**4 cup rhubarb (cut into 1/2" to 1" pieces)**

**1 1/2 cup sugar**
**1 tsp. salt**
**1 tsp. vanilla**
**1/2 cup Shortening**

## Topping:

**1/2 cup brown sugar**
**1 Tbsp. butter**

**1/4 cup white sugar**

Mix shortening and sugar, add egg, vanilla, and sour cream. Mix together salt, baking soda, and flour add to shortening mixture. Fold in rhubarb. Pour into greased 9 x 13 baking pan. Mix topping ingredients together and sprinkle over top. Bake at 350° degrees for 45 minutes.

# GERMAN APPLE CAKE

*Janet Doran*

**1 1/2 cup Crisco Oil**
**2 cup sugar**
**1 tsp. baking soda**
**1 tsp. cinnamon**
**1 tsp. lemon juice**
**1 cup chopped walnuts**
**1/2 cup butter**
**1 (8-oz.) pkg. cream cheese**
**1 (16-oz.) pkg. Confectioners sugar**
**1 tsp. vanilla**

**3 cup flour**
**3 eggs (beaten)**
**1 tsp. salt**
**1 tsp. vanilla**
**3 cups apples (sliced)**

Combine oil and sugar, set aside. Blend in eggs. In separate bowl combine flour, baking soda, salt and cinnamon, then add to oil and sugar mixture. Add vanilla and lemon juice. Add apples and nuts. Place in a greased 9 x 13 inch pan and bake for 1 hour 20 minutes at 300° degrees. If using a glass pan, shorten the baking time by 10 minutes. Combine last 4 ingredients together and beat until creamy. Frost when cake is cooled.

**Confucius say - man who sticks head in oven gets baked bean.**

# RUSSIAN POPPY SEED CAKE

*Nancy Nelson • Doris Nelson • Current Members*

1 cup ground poppy seeds
1 cup butter
3 eggs, separated
1/2 tsp. salt
2 tsp. vanilla

1 cup milk
2 cups sugar
2 cups flour
2 1/2 tsp. baking powder
powdered sugar

In a sauce pan, put poppy seeds and milk, then bring to a boil. Set aside for one hour. Cream butter and sugar. Add egg yolks and poppy seed mixture. Next add flour, salt and baking powder. In a separate bowl, beat egg whites until they are stiff. Add egg whites and vanilla to the batter. Butter and flour 2 bread pans and divide batter into them. Bake 1 hour at 350º. Check with toothpick for doneness. Sprinkle with powdered sugar when serving. Note: This is also good in a bundt pan.

# GEORGIA PECAN MIST CAKE

*Yes, you read the ingredients correctly; there is no flour in this cake.*

12 egg whites
½ teaspoon salt
3 ½ cups confectioners' sugar

3 cups pecans, finely chopped
12 egg yolks

Preheat the oven to 350º. Beat the whites and salt until foamy. Gradually add the sugar and continue to beat until stiff but not dry. Beat the yolks until thick and fold into the whites. Gently fold in the pecans. Bake in a tube pan for 50 minutes. Freezes well. Serves 16 to 20.

# RAINBOW ORANGE RAISIN CAKE

*(Extra Good) Cousin Mildred 1974*

2 eggs
1 ½ cups sugar or honey (1 cup of honey equals 2 cups of sugar • ¾ cup of honey for this recipe of 1 ½ cups sugar)
½ cup butter, melted
¼ tsp. ground nutmeg
½ cup sour milk
1 cup raisins (1/3 of a box)
1 large unpeeled orange, ground up (the whole orange)

Break eggs in mixing bowl beat until frothy. Beat in sugar and melted butter. Sift dry ingredients and add alternately with sour milk to first mixture. Fold in raisins and orange. Pour in well greased an (9x9x2 inches) and bake in preheated oven at 350º for 50 to 55 minutes. This cake is so rich it needs no frosting.

# Salt Lake City Taffy

*This is a family activity in which guests are invited to participate.*

4 cups sugar
3 cups water

1 cup white cider vinegar
2 teaspoons vanilla extract

In a heavy saucepan stir the sugar, vinegar and water together well.

Cook over high heat, stirring only once of twice until it starts boiling. Cook to 256º. Take off the stove. Add the vanilla, but do not stir. Pour on a cold greased cookie sheet. Let it cool, but stretch it as soon as possible (grease your fingers well). Lay strips of well-stretched taffy on a cabinet covered with waxed paper. Mark and cut, using cold knives. Wrap in small pieces of waxed paper. Makes 3 to 4 dozen pieces of taffy.

**Time is a great healer, but it's a lousy beautician!**

# MISSISSIPPI MUD CAKE

*Uncle Don & Aunt Betty Feb 23, 1979*

2 cups sugar
2 sticks oleo margarine
4 eggs
1 ½ cups self-rising flour
1/3 cup cocoa
3 tablespoons vanilla
1 cup chopped pecans
5 oz. miniature marshmallows

Cream sugar and oleo; add eggs and beat well. Sift flour and cocoa and add to mixture. Mix well! Add vanilla and pecans. Pour into greased and floured loaf or sheet pan. Bake 35 minutes at 325º. Remove from oven when done and put marshmallows on top. Return to oven for 10 minues at 350º. Cool for 1 hour before frosting. (See below)

## Frosting

1 box confectioner's sugar
1/3 cup cocoa
2 sticks oleo
1 tablespoon vanilla
1 cup chopped pecans
1/3 cup pet milk

Directions:

Melt oleo and add to sugar and cocoa. Mix and add milk, vanilla and pecans. Spread on cake. This cake is very good after being frozen also.

# SANDER'S BUTTER CREAM FROSTING

*Susan Badgerow*

1 cup milk
1 Tbsp. cornstarch
Beat in shaker. Stir all the time until thickens. Cool in freezer.
Next, cream til fluffy:
1 stick oleo margarine
½ cup Crisco

Beat in 1 cup sugar with the thickened goop and add 1 at a time: 1 tsp. vanilla. Beat until it looks ready for spreading.

# COCOA CAKE

*Shirley Krueger*

2/3 cup butter or oleo margarine
3 eggs
2/3 cup Hershey Cocoa
¼ tsp. baking powder
1 1/3 cup milk

1 2/3 cups sugar
2 cups sifted flour
1 ¼ tsp. baking soda
1 tsp. salt
1 tsp. vanilla

Cream butter, sugar and eggs until fluffy. Beat on high 3 minutes then reduce to low speed. Combine flour, cocoa, baking soda, baking powder, vanilla and salt, add alternately with milk to creamed mixture. Pour into 2 greased and floured 9 inch cake pans. Bake at 350º for 30 to 35 minutes.

**Forget all the health food, I need all the preservatives I can get!**

# KENTUCKY BUTTER CAKE

*Joy Thompson • 45 minutes to 1 hour*

3 cups all-purpose flour
1 teaspoon salt
2 cups sugar
4 eggs
2 teaspoons vanilla

1/2 teaspoon baking soda
1 teaspoon baking powder
1 cup butter, softened
1 cup buttermilk

1. Preheat oven to 350 degrees. Sift flour, baking soda, salt, and baking powder in medium bowl and set aside. Beat sugar and butter in a large bowl until blended. Add eggs, one at a time, beating well after each addition. Combine buttermilk with vanilla in a measuring glass.

2. Add buttermilk and flour mixtures to the large bowl (with sugar, butter, and eggs), alternating in thirds, ending with the flour mixture and beating well after each addition. Spoon batter into greased cake pans.

3. Bake until toothpick inserted in the center comes out clean, 45 minutes to 1 hour.

## BOURBON SAUCE

1/2 cup butter
1/4 cup water
Glug of bourbon

1 cup sugar
1 tablespoon vanilla

Strawberries and/or powdered sugar, optional garnish

To prepare the glaze, heat butter, sugar, water, vanilla, and bourbon in a small saucepan over medium heat until everything is melted and dissolved, about ten minutes. DO NOT BOIL.

Prick cake repeatedly with a toothpick after removing it from the oven. Pour glaze/sauce over cake and serve immediately while warm. You may want to garnish with strawberries or powdered sugar. *Source: Marriott Griffin Gate*

# CAT LITTER CAKE*

1 box spice or German chocolate cake mix
1 box of white cake mix
1 package white sandwich cookies
1 large package vanilla instant pudding mix
A few drops green food coloring
12 small Tootsie Rolls or equivalent

## SERVING "DISHES AND UTENSILS"

1 NEW cat-litter box
1 NEW cat-litter box liner
1 NEW pooper scooper

Prepare and bake cake mixes, according to directions, in any size pan.
Prepare pudding and chill.
Crumble cookies in small batches in a blender or food processor.
Add a few drops of green food coloring to 1 cup of cookie crumbs.
Mix with a fork or shake in a jar. Set aside.
When cakes are at room temperature, crumble them into a large bowl. Toss with half of the remaining cookie crumbs and enough pudding to make the mixture moist but not soggy.
Place liner in litter box and pour in mixture.
Unwrap 3 Tootsie Rolls and heat in a microwave until soft and pliable. Shape the blunt ends into slightly curved points. Repeat with three more rolls. Bury the rolls decoratively in the cake mixture. Sprinkle remaining white cookie crumbs over the mixture, then scatter green crumbs lightly over top.
Heat 5 more Tootsie Rolls until almost melted. Scrape them on top of the cake and sprinkle with crumbs from the litter box. Heat the remaining Tootsie Roll until pliable and hang it over the edge of the box.
Place litter box on a sheet of newspaper and serve with scooper.    *This is a real recipe.

**Laughing helps, its like jogging on the inside.**                77

# FRUITCAKE # 1...

*by Joan Atkins Sault Sainte Marie, MI*
*Recipe of Margaret Atkins (my mother-in-law)*

## Our wedding cake...

12 eggs
2 # currants
1 # lard
1 pint sour cream
walnut meats

5 # raisins
1 # brown sugar
about 3 cups of flour
1/2 pint molasses

1/2 cup spices....(cinnamon, nutmeg, cloves and allspice)
1 # dates or sticky raisins, cherries and pineapple

Mix all ingredients. Grease pans, line with brown paper (or parchment) and grease again. Bake in slow oven at 275 degrees.

I put dish of water in the oven while baking, to keep moist.

When cooled, I soak cheesecloth in cherry brandy and wrap fruitcake. Put it in foil or plastic bags...Freezes very well.

# FRUITCAKE # 2...

*by Joan Atkins Sault Sainte Marie, MI*
*Recipe belongs to my Aunt Lila*

## JEWELED FRUITCAKE....

2 eggs
1 jar mincemeat
2 cups mixed candied fruit

1/2 cup water
2 pkg. date bread mix
1 cup chopped nuts

Preheat oven to 350 degrees. Grease and flour 10 inch tube or bundt pan.

In large bowl, combine the eggs and water. Stir in the mincemeat, date bread mixes, candied fruit and nuts. Pour into pan. Bake 80 to 90 minutes or until toothpick comes out clean. Cool 15 minutes. Turn onto rack; cool. Drizzle with a powdered sugar glaze if desired. Top with candied fruit for decoration.

*I like using mixed candied cherries and pineapple instead of the mixed fruit...(just me)...*
*Hope you enjoy! Joan Atkins*

**The most dangerous food of all is a wedding cake.**

## OLD-FASHIONED BANANA PUDDING

*There are dozens of recipes for banana pudding, but this is the one that's the classic.*

**One 12-oz. box of vanilla wafers**
**1/2 cup unsifted cornstarch**
**2/3 cup sugar**
**1/4 teaspoon salt**
**3 cups whole milk**
**3 eggs**
**1 teaspoon vanilla extract**
**2 tablespoons (1/4 stick) butter, cut up**
**5 perfectly ripe bananas**
**1 cup whipping cream, whipped with 1/4 cup confectioners' sugar**

1. Line the bottom and sides of a 13 by 9-inch glass casserole with about half of the vanilla wafers.

2. Mix the cornstarch, sugar, and salt in the top of a double boiler. Slowly add the milk and cook over simmering water until the mixture is thick, 12 to 15 minutes, stirring constantly.

3. Beat the eggs in a small heatproof glass dish and add about 1/4 cup of the hot milk mixture to the eggs. Stir, then add the eggs to the double boiler. Cook for 1 minute more. (The custard should be about the consistency of mayonnaise. If it is not, keep stirring over simmering water until it thickens.) Add the vanilla and butter and stir until combined. Turn off the heat, transfer the custard to a bowl, place a piece of plastic wrap directly on the pudding to prevent a skin from forming, and allow the pudding to cool to room temperature.

4. Slice a generous layer of bananas over the vanilla wafers. Cover with about half the pudding. Repeat the layers - vanilla wafers, bananas, and pudding. Top with a thick layer of whipped cream. Serve at room temperature, or cover with plastic wrap and chill.

Serves 10 to 12.

**Coffee makes it possible to get out of bed, chocolate makes it worthwhile.** 79

# BAHAMIAN BREAD PUDDING

3 cups bread, cut in cubes about ½" square
3 cups milk
3 eggs
¾ cup sugar
1 Tbsp. baking powder
3 Tbsp. butter, melted
1 Tbsp. cinnamon
1 Tbsp. vanilla
½ tsp. nutmeg
1 cup raisins
Dash of salt

Preheat oven to 350° degrees F. Soak bread cubes in milk for 5 minutes. Beat eggs in a large mixing bowl. Add bread, milk and remaining ingredients and mix well. Pour into a 2-quart buttered baking dish. Set baking dish into a pan of hot water in oven. Bake for 1 hour or until pudding sets. Makes 6 to 8 servings.

# RICE PUDDING

3 cup cooked rice
2 cups milk
1/8 tsp. salt
1/3 cup sugar
1 Tbls. butter
1 beaten egg
grated lemon rind
1/4 cup raisins

Mix rice well with rest of ingredients. Bake 20 minutes in a buttered baking dish.

# BANANA PUDDING WITH MERINGUE

*You will find this every day at dessert time at Mrs. Wilkes'. "For a delicious change, we sometimes substitute our pound cake for the vanilla wafers," informs Marcia. This is a special favorite of the Girl Scouts who troop over from the Juliette Gordon Low House, birthplace of the founder of the Girl Scouts of America.*

1 (6-ounce) box instant vanilla pudding
1 (7 ¼ -ounce) box vanilla wafers
4 bananas, sliced
Meringue (recipe follows)

Preheat the oven to 375°. Make the pudding according to the directions on the box. Arrange the wafers, sliced bananas, and pudding in layers in a 2-quart casserole, ending with a layer of pudding on top. This will make 3 layers. Spread the meringue gently over the top. Bake for 15 minutes. Serves 8.

NOTE: For a quicker version of this recipe, use pudding as directed on box and place a layer of whipped cream on top.

# MERINGUE

2 egg whites
4 tablespoons sugar
1/8 teaspoon salt
¼ teaspoon vanilla extract

Beat the egg whites and salt until frothy. Add 1 tablespoon of sugar at a time and vanilla and beat until the meringue is stiff.

**I used to work in a blanket factory, but it folded.**

# FABULOUS FUDGE

2 ¼ cups sugar
¾ cup evaporated milk
1 cup Marshmallow Crème or 16 large
marshmallows
¼ cup butter or margarine
¼ tsp. salt
1 pkg. ( 6 oz) Semi-sweet
  Chocolate Morsels
1 tsp. vanilla extract
1 cup chopped nuts

In a heavy **2-quart saucepan,** mix together the sugar, evaporated milk, marshmallow crème or marshmallows, butter and salt.

Cook, stirring constantly, over medium heat to a boil (mixture will be bubbling all over top). Boil and stir until the mixture registers 236° F on a **candy thermometer** or about 4 to 5 minutes. Remove from heat.

Stir in the chocolate morsels until completely melted. Stir in the extract and the nuts. Spread in a buttered **8-inch square pan**. Cool and cut into 30 pieces.

# EASY FUDGE

*Submitted by Katy Salutes • Hamburg, MI*

2 cups semi-sweet chocolate chips
1 can sweetened condensed milk
Dash of salt

1 cup milk chocolate chips
1 1/2 tsp. vanilla
3/4 cup chopped walnuts

1. Line 8 or 9 inch square pan with waxed paper.
2. Combine first 5 ingredients in a heavy pan, and cook over medium heat until melted.
3. Remove from heat and add walnuts. Spread evenly into prepared pan, and refrigerate for about 2 hours.
4. Remove from pan, peel off waxed paper and cut into squares.

# FUDGE SICKLES

*Submitted by Joann Schmidt - Chesaning, MI*

1 box dark chocolate instant pudding
1/3 cup sugar
1 can evaporated milk

Put in blender, then in popsicle container. Freeze.

# MAMIE EISENHOWER'S MILLION DOLLAR FUDGE

Makes 5 lbs.
4 ½ cups sugar
1-13 oz. can evaporated milk
1-12 oz. package semi-sweet chocolate bits
3-12 oz packages German Sweet Chocolate
1-8 oz. jar marshmallow cream

2 Tbsp. butter
pinch of salt

2 cups chopped nuts

Boil together sugar, butter and milk and pinch of salt for 6 minutes. Pour syrup into large bowl over chocolate bits, chocolate and marshmallow cream. Add nuts. Beat until chocolate is melted. Pour into buttered 13x9x2-inch pan. Let stand several hours before cutting.

**Some minds are like concrete, thoroughly mixed and permanently set.** 81

## BEIGNET RECIPE

1 cup lukewarm water
1/4 cup sugar
1/2 teaspoon salt
1 egg, room temperature & beaten
2 tablespoons butter, softened
1/2 cup evaporated milk
4 cups bread flour or all-purpose flour
3 teaspoons instant active dry yeast
Vegetable oil*
Powdered sugar for dusting

*Use just enough vegetable oil to completely cover beignets while frying.

Using a mixer with a dough hook, place water, sugar, salt, egg, butter, evaporated milk, flour, and yeast in the bowl. Beat until smooth. If using a bread machine, select dough setting and press Start. When dough cycle has finished, remove dough from pan and turn out onto a lightly oiled surface. Form dough into an oval, place in a lightly greased bowl, cover with plastic wrap, and refrigerate until well chilled (3 to 4 hours) or overnight.

To prepare dough, remove from refrigerator and roll out on a lightly floured board to 1/2-inch thickness. Cut into approximately 3-inch squares or circles.

In a deep fryer or large pot, heat vegetable oil to 360 degrees F. Fry the beignets (2 or 3 at a time) 2 to 3 minutes or until they are puffed and golden brown on both sides, turning them in the oil with tongs once or twice to get them evenly brown; beignets will rise to the surface of the oil as soon as they begin to puff. NOTE: If the beignets don't rise to the top immediately when dropped into the oil, the oil is not hot enough. Remove from oil and drain on paper towels, then sprinkle heavily with powdered sugar. Serve hot.

*NOTE: The dough can be kept for up to a week in the refrigerator - it actually improves with age; just punch down when it rises. Dough can also be frozen; cut and roll, or shape doughnuts before freezing.)* Makes 18 beignets.

## PECAN PIE MUFFINS

*These are great on any brunch table, and to bring along on picnics, too.*

1/2 cup (1 stick) butter, softened
3/4 cup packed light brown sugar
2 eggs, beaten
1/2 cup all-purpose flour
3/4 cup chopped pecans

1. Preheat the oven to 350ºF. Grease and flour 8 muffin tin cups or use paper liners

2. In a medium bowl, cream the butter and sugar. Add the eggs and mix well. Add the flour and stir until just combined. Stir in the pecans.

3. Spoon the batter into the prepared muffin cups, filling about two-thirds full.

4. Bake for 25 minutes. Serve warm with more butter! Makes 8 muffins

**Middle age is when you choose the cereal for the fiber, not the toy.**

# DUTCH OVEN PEACH COBBLER

Campers from other sites come driving over to see what's cooking when they smell this cinnamon peach cobbler. Sometimes, Mr. English adds fresh blueberries. Be sure to share! It's the southern thing to do!

**2 (16 oz.) cans sliced peaches in heavy or light syrup, or in fruit juice, your choice.**
**1 pint fresh blueberries (optional)**
**½ cup Bisquick baking mix**
**1/3 cup sugar**
**Ground cinnamon**

Spray a Dutch oven with vegetable oil cooking spray. Drain 1 can of peaches. Combine both cans of peaches, including the juice from the undrained can, the blueberries, if using, the Bisquick, sugar, and a sprinkling of cinnamon. Place with mixture into the Dutch oven.

## Topping:

**2¼ cups Bisquick baking mix**
**¼ cup (1/2 stick) butter, melted**
**Cinnamon sugar**

**¼ cup sugar**
**½ cup milk**

Combine the Bisquick, sugar, butter, and milk in a re-sealable plastic bag. Using your fingers, drop bits of Topping on top of the peaches. Sprinkle with cinnamon sugar. Place the Dutch oven over about 12 coals, then cover with lid; place about 12 coals on top. Check in 10 minutes; if the dough is brown, there are too many coals on top. If it is not brown at all, add a few coals. The cobbler usually cooks in 30 minutes. Serves about 10 hungry campers.

**Dachshunds are great for kids, they already come stretched and pulled.**

# P&J RICE KRISPIE TREATS

3 tablespoons  butter or margarine
1 package  (10 oz., about 40) regular marshmallows
 - OR -
4 cups miniature marshmallows
1/2 cup peanut butter
6 cups  Rice Krispies®

*Stovetop Directions:*
1. In large saucepan melt butter over low heat. Add marshmallows and stir until completely melted. Remove from heat. Stir in peanut butter until melted.
2. Add KELLOGG'S RICE KRISPIES cereal. Stir until well coated.
3. Using buttered spatula or wax paper, evenly press mixture into 13 x 9 x 2-inch pan coated with cooking spray. Cool. Cut into 2-inch squares. Best if served the same day.
*Microwave Directions:*
In microwave-safe bowl heat butter and marshmallows on HIGH for 3 minutes, stirring after 2 minutes.

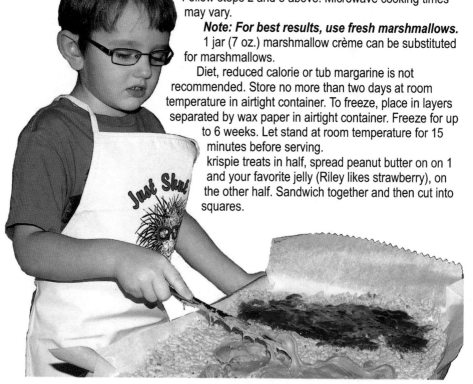

Stir until smooth. Add peanut butter, stirring until combined. Follow steps 2 and 3 above. Microwave cooking times may vary.

**Note: For best results, use fresh marshmallows.**
1 jar (7 oz.) marshmallow crème can be substituted for marshmallows.
Diet, reduced calorie or tub margarine is not recommended. Store no more than two days at room temperature in airtight container. To freeze, place in layers separated by wax paper in airtight container. Freeze for up to 6 weeks. Let stand at room temperature for 15 minutes before serving.
krispie treats in half, spread peanut butter on on 1 and your favorite jelly (Riley likes strawberry), on the other half. Sandwich together and then cut into squares.

# DATE TORTE
*Grandma Oleta Lindenberg*

**3 heaping tablespoons of flour**
**1 teaspoon baking powder**
**3/4 cup brown sugar**
**2 eggs, well beaten**
**1 teaspoon vanilla**
**1 cup walnuts**
**1 cup dates**
**1/4 teaspoon salt**
   Bake in 350° degree oven for 20 minutes.

# PUFF BALL DOUGHNUTS

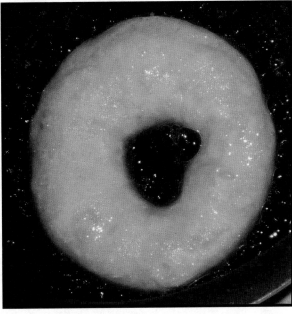

**3 eggs**
**1 cup sugar**
**1 pint milk**
**pinch of salt**
**1/2 tsp. nutmeg**
**4 - 5 cups flour**
**2 heaping tsp. baking powder**
   These doughnuts are eaten fresh and warm, are a delicious breakfast dish and are quickly made. Beat eggs slightly, add sugar, milk, salt, and nutmeg. Whisk together, add enough flour to allow a spoon to stand up in the batter. Add baking powder; beat together until very light. Drop by spoonfuls into boiling oil. Remove when browned. These cakes will not absorb a bit of fat and are not at all rich, and consequently are the least injurious of these kind of cakes.

# EASY LEMON SUGAR SNAPS
*Gloria Kirchman • Eden Prairie, MN*

**3/4 cup butter, softened**
**1 egg**
**1 pkg. 2-layer-size lemon cake mix**
**1 cup yellow cornmeal**
**2 Tbsp. finely shredded lemon peel**
**Coarse sugar or granulated sugar**
   Preheat oven to 375° degrees F. In a large mixing bowl, beat butter and egg with an electric mixer on medium to high speed for 30 seconds. Gradually beat in cake mix until combined; stir in cornmeal and lemon peel.
   Using 1 tablespoon of dough for each cookie, roll into 1-inch balls. Roll in sugar. Place 2 inches apart on ungreased cookie sheets. Bake for 9 to 10 minutes or until bottoms are lightly browned. Let cool on cookie sheet for 1 minute. Transfer to wire rack. Cool completely. Makes about 3 1/2 dozen cookies.

**Black holes is where God divided by zero.**

## PLANTATION BARS "COLORADO"
*Submitted by Joann Schmidt - Chesaning, MI*

1-1/2 lb. white chocolate almond bark
1-1/2 cup Peanut butter
2 c. dry roasted peanuts
1 pkg. mini marshmallows
4 to 6 cups rice krispies

Melt almond bark in microwave, stir in peanut butter, the peanuts, then the marshmallows. Just make sure you stir after every item. Refrigerate to set.   (Freezes very well)

## GOOEY BUTTERSCOTCH BUBBLE LOAF
*Cheryl Shantz*

12 frozen dinner rolls, thawed, but still cold
1 small box (non-instant) butterscotch pudding mix
1/2-1 cup chopped pecans or walnuts
1 1/4 cup butter or margarine
1/2 cup brown sugar

Spray loaf pan with non-stick cooking spray, cut rolls in half and roll in dry pudding mix. Arrange in pan alternately with nuts. Sprinkle remaining pudding mix over the top. Combine brown sugar and butter, heat together until butter is melted and syrup is formed.  Stir well. Pour syrup over rolls. Cover with sprayed plastic wrap. Let rise until double. Remove wrap, bake at 350° degrees for 30-35 minutes. Do not under bake.

Immediately invert onto a serving platter.

## PEANUT BUTTER BALLS
*Cricket LeCross*

1 cup Peanut Butter
6 Tbsp. Softened Butter
2 cup Powdered Sugar
Chocolate Almond Bark

Mix peanut butter and butter. Gradually add sugar, mixing well until combined. Shape into 1" balls, place on waxed paper. Let stand about 20 minutes until dry. Melt almond bark in microwave safe bowl. Using toothpick, dip ball into coating one at a time and let excess drip off. Place on waxed paper. Let stand until coating is dry.

TIP: Touch the top of each ball with another peanut butter ball to cover a bare spot on the top. Does not need to be refrigerated unless in high heat areas.

## PECAN PUFFS
*Vicki Carlson*

1/2 cup Butter or Margarine
1 tsp. Vanilla
1 cup Sifted Cake Flour

2 Tbsp. Sugar
1 cup Pecan Meats
Powdered Sugar

Beat butter until soft, add sugar and beat until creamy, add vanilla.  Stir in pecan meats and cake flour.  Roll dough into small balls and place on greased cookie sheet. Bake about 30 minutes.  Roll in powdered sugar while still warm.

**I finally got my head together and my body fell apart.**

# BOW'S BAKED CUSTARD

*Bow Ross*

Here is a new recipe direct from Bow Ross, not from her cookbook. Bow writes that "This is delicious! At least that's the opinion of my friends!"

**3 eggs**
**8 oz. milk**
**8 oz. half & half**
**1/4 cup sugar**
**1 tsp. vanilla**
**Grated nutmeg**

Put all ingredients in blender, except nutmeg. Blend on high speed for 30 seconds. Pour into a 3 cup baking dish. Dust the top with hand grated nutmeg and place in a pan of water. Bake at 300° for 1 1/4 hours, then let set in oven for another 15 minutes.

## GUAVA DUFF

*A true Bahamian delicacy. If you think the guava might be difficult to find at home, buy some in a supermarket specialty store.*

**1 lb. guava jam**
**½ tsp. salt & 1/2 tsp. sugar**
**3 oz. Crisco**

**10 oz. Bisquick**
**4 oz. margarine or butter**
**1 cup white flour**

Mix together Bisquick, salt, white flour and sugar. Into this mixture cut in margarine or butter and Crisco. Cut in gradually about 2 Tbsp. iced water until pastry reaches consistency. With rolling pin roll out ¾ inch thick so that width is the length of a loaf pan. Spread with jam 1 inch inside edges. Moisten edges, roll up with width-wide, pinching edges together. Place in greased loaf pan, paint top with milk and sprinkle on a little sugar. Bake in 350 degree F. oven for ¾ hour or until sides and top are browned. Slice and serve, while still slightly warm.

## TOFFEE APPLE BARS

*Phyllis Baker*

**2 cup flour**
**1 cup butter or oleo**
**1 egg**
**1/2 tsp. cinnamon**
**1 cup chopped pecans**
**1 cup powdered sugar**

**1/2 cup powdered sugar**
**1 can sweetened condensed milk**
**1 tsp. vanilla**
**1 cup apple (chopped fine)**
**1 cup toffee bits**
**2 to 4 Tbsp. maple syrup**

Combine flour, 1/2 cup powdered sugar and butter. Cut butter until it has coarse crumbs. Press crumbs into ungreased 9x13-inch pan. Bake at 350° for 15 minutes. In large bowl combine milk, egg, vanilla and cinnamon. Mix well. Add apple, pecans and toffee bits. Pour over crust. Bake 30 minutes at 350°. Run knife around sides. Cool. Mix 1 cup powdered sugar and maple syrup. Drizzle over bars. Delicious!

**Wear short sleeves! Support your right to bare arms!**

# PEANUT BUTTER COOKIES
*Doris 1990*

Sift together:
**1 ¼ cup flour**
**¼ tsp. baking soda**
Cream together:
**½ cups shorting**
**½ cup peanut butter**
**½ cup brown sugar**
**½ cup white sugar**
**1 egg**
Mix together and drop on parchment paper on cookie sheet.
Bake at 350° 12-15 minutes.

## BAKED RICE PUDDING
*Opal's recipe*
Makes 6 servings
Combine in a saucepan:
**2/3 cups minute rice**
**2 ¾ cups milk**
**½ cup sugar**
**1 tsp. salt**
**½ cup raisins**
Bring to a boil stirring often. Reduce heat and simmer 10 minutes.

Mix
**2 slightly beaten eggs**
**1 tsp. vanilla**
**1 tsp. nutmeg**
Place in a greased pan, set that pan in a larger pan half filled in water. Bake at 375° for 20 minutes or until knife comes out clean from center.

## MOTHER KRUEGERS "SLUNGUDEN"
*9-13-1932*

**1 lb. walnut meats**
**1 lb. Graham crackers**
**1 lb. marshmallows**
**1 lb. pitted dates**
**1 can evaporated milk**
**Whipped cream**
Grind together first 4 ingredients and put in pan. Mix with can of milk until firm. Make into meat loaf style.
Put in refrigerator til firm. Cut in slices and top with whipped cream.

**If everything seems to be going well, you have obviously overlooked something.**

# CHOCOLATE TRUFFLES

YIELD: 24 - 25 calorie truffles

*Submitted by Paulin Reedy, of Hagerstown, Maryland*

INGREDIENTS:
**2 cups graham cracker crumbs**
**1/3 cup unsweetened cocoa**
**powder**
**6 tablespoons evaporated skim**
**milk**
**¼ cup water**
**1 teaspoon vanilla extract**
PREPARATION:
Combine crumbs and cocoa powder. In a separate bowl, combine milk, water and vanilla. Stir milk mixture into cocoa mixture. It will be crumbly. Turn dough onto a work surface and knead until it holds together. Roll dough into a 12 inch rope. Divide into 24 equal pieces. Roll each piece into a ball. Dust lightly with confectioner's sugar before serving.

# JEWISH COFFEE CAKE

*"The Best" Doris-My Sister 7-29-1972*

**6 eggs**
**½ lb. oleo**
**2 cups sugar**
**4 cups flour**
**½ tsp. salt**
**1 tsp. soda**
**1 ½ tsp. baking powder**
**1 tsp. vanilla**
**1 pint sour cream**
Cream:
Oleo, sugar and eggs.
Sift flour add soda, salt and baking powder. Add to creamed mixture. Then add vanilla. Mix thoroughly. Fold in sour cream.
Filling:
½ cup light brown sugar
1 tsp. cinnamon
1 cup ground nuts
Butter an angel food pan. Pour in about 1/3 batter, then some filling, more batter and then filling, remainder of batter. Leave very little of filling for the top. Bake at 350° for 1 hour and 15 minutes.

**I wish the buck stopped here, as I could use a few.**

# Here are a Few Helpful Household Hints

**Reheat Pizza** • Heat up leftover pizza in a nonstick skillet on top of the stove, set heat to med-low and heat till warm. This keeps the crust crispy. No soggy micro pizza.

**Easy Deviled Eggs** • Put cooked egg yolks in a Ziplock bag. Seal, mash till they are all broken up. Add remainder of ingredients, reseal, keep mashing it up mixing thoroughly, cut the tip of the baggy, squeeze mixture into egg. Just throw bag away when done, easy clean up.

**Expanding Frosting** • When you buy a container of cake frosting from the store, whip it with your mixer for a few minutes. You can double it in size. You get to frost more cake/cupcakes with the same amount. You also eat less sugar and calories per serving.

**Reheating Refrigerated Bread** • To warm biscuits, pancakes, or muffins that were refrigerated, place them in a microwave with a cup of water. The increased moisture will keep the food moist and help it reheat faster.

**Broken Glass** • Use a wet cotton ball or Q-tip to pick up the small shards of glass you can't see easily.

**No More Mosquitoes** • Place a dryer sheet in your pocket. It will keep the mosquitoes away.

**Squirrel Away** • To keep squirrels from eating your plants, sprinkle your plants with cayenne pepper. The cayenne pepper doesn't hurt the plant and the squirrels won't come near it.

**Flexible vacuum** • To get something out of a heat register or under the fridge add an empty paper towel roll or empty gift wrap roll to your vacuum. It can be bent or flattened to get in narrow openings.

**Reducing Static Cling** • Pin a small safety pin to the seam of your slip and you will not have a clingy skirt or dress. Same thing works with slacks that cling when wearing panty hose. Place pin in seam of slacks and * ta da! -- static is gone.

**Measuring Cups** • Before you pour sticky substances into a measuring cup, fill with hot water. Dump out the hot water, but don't dry cup. Next, add your ingredient, such as peanut butter, and watch how easily it comes right out.

**Foggy Windshield** • Hate foggy windshields? Buy a chalkboard eraser and keep it in the glove box of your car. When the windows fog, rub with the eraser! Works better than a cloth!

**Reopening an envelope** • If you seal an envelope and then realize you forgot to include something inside, just place your sealed envelope in the freezer for an hour or two. Viola! It unseals easily.

**Conditioner** • Use your hair conditioner to shave your legs. It's a lot cheaper than shaving cream and leaves your legs really smooth. It's also a great way to use up the conditioner you bought but didn't like when you tried it in your hair.

**Goodbye Fruit Flies** • To get rid of pesky fruit flies, take a small glass, fill it 1/2" with Apple Cider Vinegar and 2 drops of dish washing liquid, mix well. You will find those flies drawn to the cup and gone forever!

**Get Rid of Ants** • Put small piles of cornmeal where you see ants. They eat it, take it "home", can't digest it so it kills them. It may take a week or so, especially if it rains, but it works & you don't have the worry about pets or small children being harmed!

**The nicest things about the future is it always starts tomorrow.**

# BACON SALAD DRESSING

**8 strips lean bacon**
**1 cup sugar**
**½ cup water**
**¾ cup red wine vinegar**
**1 teaspoon salt (or to taste)**

Fry bacon, drain and crumble. Pour bacon grease into saucepan. Add remaining ingredients. Keep warm until served. Do not prepare ahead because grease will solidify. Serves 8-10

*Serve on spinach or other salad greens for a wilted salad.*

## CANDIED WALNUTS

*Yield: 2 servings*
**1/3 cup walnuts**
**2 tablespoons maple syrup**

1. Preheat oven to 300°F

2. Mix the walnuts and the maple syrup. Spread the walnut mixture on a baking sheet and bake for 10 to 12 minutes. Cool and reserve for garnish.

## FRENCH SALAD DRESSING

**2 cans tomato soup (1 lb 4 oz) each**
**1 heaping tablespoon garlic salt**
**1 heaping tablespoon celery salt**
**1 ¾ oz. onion flakes**
**½ cup sugar**
**½ cup vinegar**

**½ cup oil**
**Juice of one lemon**

Mix all. Let sit at room temperature 2 or 3 hours – stir now and then.

**The secret of a happy marriage will always remain a secret.**

# TROPICAL SALSA

½ cup mango, chopped
½ cup banana, chopped
½ cup fresh orange, peeled and chopped
½ cup purple onion, finely chopped
1 ½ tsp. fresh Jalapeño pepper, seeded & minced
1 Tbsp. cilantro, minced
1 tsp. brown sugar
1/8 tsp. cinnamon

Combine all ingredients, stirring gently. Makes about 1 ¼ cups.

# RUM SAUCE

½ cup butter
1 cup white sugar
¼ cup rum
Grated nutmeg

Cream butter and sugar together until light and smooth. Add rum a little at a time. Continue beating until very fluffy. Serve over bread pudding with a sprinkle of grated nutmeg on top of sauce. Makes about 1 cup.

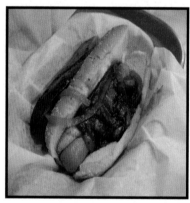

# ZIPPY ONION RELISH

*From Jack's Cosmic Dogs*

3 large onions, chopped
1/2 cup tomato sauce
3 Tbsp. catsup
2 Tbsp. water
1 1/2 tsp. sugar
1/2 tsp. dried oregano
1/4 tsp. salt
1/4 tsp. garlic salt
1/4 tsp. crushed pepper

Saute 20 minutes. Adds zip to any Hot Dog!

# AUNT CAROLYN'S CONEY SAUCE

*from Carolyn Potter – Sandpoint*

½ lb. ground beef
¼ cup onion, chopped
1 tsp. garlic powder or garlic clove
½ tsp. chili powder
¼ cup water
12 tsp. Accent
8 oz. can tomato sauce
½ tsp. salt.

Combine all and simmer for 1 hour. Freeze in small cups for 2 hot dogs.

# GRAM'S SPICY SAUCE:

4 oz. butter
1 clove garlic, minced
½ teaspoon dry mustard
2 tablespoons chopped onion
2 teaspoons Worcestershire sauce
1 dash Tabasco sauce (optional)

Melt the butter in a frying pan and add the onions and garlic, fry until soft.
Add the rest of the ingredients and heat sauce til warm, pour over your choice
of meat for a tasty sauce or marinade.

**Remember . . . . when nobody was prettier than your mom?**

# SMOOTH BOURBON SAUCE:

*From Jim's (Hangman's Army Mystic, IA) friend Bill Pelton, Canyon Lake, TX*

**2/3 cup of Bourbon (your choice!)**
**¾ stick unsalted butter – cut into pieces for faster melting**
**¼ finely chopped shallots**
**2/3 cup beef stock or canned beef broth**

Melt the butter and add shallots in a saucepan. Cook shallots on low heat in butter until soft. Add the beef stock and the Bourbon to the saucepan, heat and use to your liking.

## CONEY ISLANDS
*Outdoor appetites? Count on 2 Coneys apiece*

**12 frankfurters, heated**
**12 coney buns, heated**
**Prepared mustard**
**Chopped onion**
**1 recipe Coney Sauce**

Set everything out, help yourself style. Folks place franks in buns, smear on mustard, spoon on onion, then hot Coney Sauce.

*Makes 12 Coneys*

To heat franks for picnic: Preheat a wide-mouth vacuum or insulated jug by filling with boiling water; let stand few minutes. Empty; refill jug almost to top

with boiling water, leaving space for franks; add lid. When your picnickers are hungry, add franks to jug; let heat in the water, with lid on, for 7 to 10 minutes. Remove franks from water with tongs.

## CONEY SAUCE
*Long jaunt or boat trip? Take cans of chili con carne instead. (Also canned franks)*

**1/2 pound ground beef**
**1/4 cup water**
**1/4 cup chopped onions**
**1 clove garlic, minced**
**1 8-oz. can (1 cup) seasoned tomato sauce**
**1/2 to 3/4 teaspoon chili powder**
**1/2 teaspoon monosodium glutamate (MSG), optional**
**1/2 teaspoon salt**

Brown ground beef slowly but thoroughly, breaking with fork till fine. Add remaining ingredients; simmer uncovered 10 minutes. Makes sauce for 12 Coneys.

**Friends are like wine, they get better with age.**

# CHEESE AND BACON APPETIZERS

Prep Time: 10 minutes    Baking Time: 20 minutes   Broiling time: 2 minutes

**10 bread slices, preferably homemade type**
**1  8 oz. pkg. sharp cheddar cheese**
**1 egg**
**4 Tbsp. heavy cream**
**freshly ground pepper**
**dash of nutmeg**
**2 Tbsp. chopped parsley**
**8 slices lean bacon**

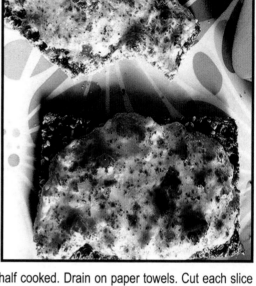

1. Prepare appetizer croutons. Trim crusts from bread slices, cut slices into quarters. Place bread pieces on baking sheet, bake in 250° degree oven 20 minutes or until lightly browned and very dry.

2. Prepare cheese spread. Place cheese, egg, cream, nutmeg, and pepper to taste in blender container. Blend mixture until perfectly smooth and homogeneous. Transfer to a bowl and fold in parsley.

2. Slowly fry or microwave bacon until half cooked. Drain on paper towels. Cut each slice into 5 pieces.

4. Spread cheese mixture on toast pieces, top each with bacon piece. Place toast on baking sheet. Broil for 2 minutes or until hot, puffed and bubbling. Serve hot from broiler.  Makes 40 canapes.

# ARTICHOKE DIP AU GRATIN

**1 garlic clove**
**1 cup mayonnaise**
**1/4 tsp. cayenne pepper**
**white pepper to taste**
**2 Tbsp. grated parmesan cheese**
**1  14 oz. can artichoke hearts**
**paprika**

1. Chop garlic clove very fine, blend with small amount of mayonnaise until well incorporated, combine with remaining mayonnaise, cayenne pepper, white pepper and parmesan cheese.

2. Chop drained artichoke hearts into small pieces, fold into mayonnaise mixture. Stir until well combined.

3. Pour mixture into ovenproof casserole. (The gratin will rise at lease one inch while baking). Sprinkle top of gratin with paprika. Bake in 350° degree oven for 20 minutes or until bubbling.

4. Serve warm with crusty French bread or as a dip with broken toasted tortillas.

# BLUE MOTORCYCLE
*Bruce Black*

1/2 oz. Blue Curacao
1/2 oz. rum

1/2 oz. sour mix
1/2 oz. triple sec

Blend all ingredients with ice and serve with an orange slice and a cherry.

# THE BEST BUTTERY DILL PRETZELS
*"The Pretzel Princess" Cricket LeCross*

**2 large bags pretzel thins?? (Is there such a thing)**
**1 bottle Orville Redenbacher Popcorn Oil**
**1 envelope dry ranch dressing**
**1 tsp. garlic powder**
**1 Tbsp. dill weed**

Pour bags of pretzels into gallon sized bags (1 each) Mix oil, dressing, garlic, and dill weed together in medium bowl. Pour half of mixture into each bag of pretzels. Turn bags continuously until mixture is absorbed into pretzels, or, till your arm falls off... Tastes Great!!!

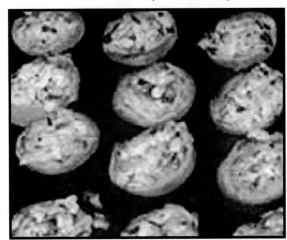

## ARTICHOKE BRUSCHETTA
*Libby McMillan*

**1- 6.5 oz. jar marinated artichoke hearts, drained and chopped**
**1/2 C. grated Romano cheese**
**1/3 C. finely chopped red onion**
**5 Tbsp. mayo**
**1 French baguette, cut into 1/3" slices**

Mix first four ingredients and spread on bread slices. Broil in preheated oven 2 minutes or until toppings are bubble and lightly brown. Simple and a crowd pleaser!

# SMOKY BACON WRAPS
*Caroline Souva*

**1 lb. sliced bacon**
**1 pkg. miniature smoked sausage links**
**1 cup packed brown sugar**

Cut each bacon strip in half widthwise. Wrap one piece of bacon around each sausage. Place in a foil-lined 15x10" baking pan. Sprinkle with brown sugar. Bake, uncovered, at 400° for 30 to 40 minutes or until bacon is crisp and sausage is heated through.

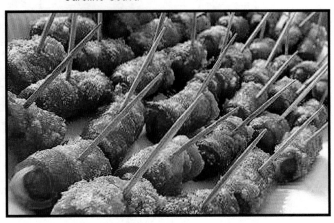

**Money isn't everything, but it sure keeps the kids in touch.**

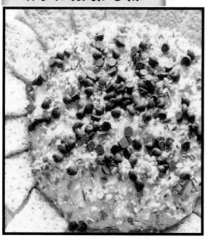

# CHOCOLATE CHIP CHEESE BALL
*Kris McGill*

1-8 oz. cream cheese, room temp.
1 stick butter, room temp.
1/4 tsp. vanilla
3/4 cup powdered sugar
2 Tbsp. brown sugar
3/4 cup mini-chocolate chips
1/2 cup chopped pecans or
      sundae topping nuts

Mix cream cheese, butter & vanilla with mixer until smooth; add brown sugar & powdered sugar. Fold in by hand mini-chocolate chips. Refrigerate for 2 hours, then shape in ball and roll in nuts. Refrigerate until ready to use. Serve with Nabisco graham cracker sticks.

# PINEAPPLE CHEESE SPREAD
*Debbie Ramey*

2-8 oz. pkgs. cream cheese, softened
1-8 1/2 oz. can crushed pineapple, drained
1/3 cup plus 1 cup. chopped pecans, divided use
1/4 cup chopped green pepper
2 Tbsp. chopped green onion
1 tsp. seasoned salt

In bowl place cream cheese; gradually stir in crushed pineapple, 1/3 cup pecans, green onions, green pepper and seasoning salt. Cover; chill several hours. Form into a ball, then roll in additional 1 cup of pecans. Serve with any brand of butter-flavored crackers. Makes 1 1/2 cups

# SPINACH DIP
*Ev Hellebuyck*

2 cup sour cream
1/2 cup mayonnaise
1 pkg. Knorr vegetable soup mix
2 cup raw chopped spinach
Green onions, chopped
    (as many as desired)
1 round loaf of bread

Mix all ingredients together. Cut hole in center of bread, taking out excess. Fill with dip. Use bread that was removed to dip into.

# BEER MUFFINS
*Ev Hellebuyck*

4 cup Bisquick
5 Tbsp. sugar
1-12 oz. can or bottle beer, chilled

In a large bowl, combine Bisquick and sugar; mix well. Gradually add beer and stir until well combined. Divide batter equally in well greased 12-count muffin tin. Bake at 350° for 40 - 45 minutes, or until muffins are large and puffy and lightly browned on top. Makes 12 muffins.

**I used to have a handle on life but it broke.**

# MAPLE BARBECUE SAUCE

*Armande Trembley*
*- St. Albans, VT*

**1 cup ketchup**
**1 cup pure Vermont maple syrup**
**1/4 cup soy sauce**
**1/4 cup vinegar**
**1/4 cup finely chopped onion**
**1/4 cup finely chopped Granny Smith apple**
**1/4 cup minced garlic**
**2 Tbsp. pepper**
**2 tsp. ginger**
**2 tsp. cajun seasoning**

Mix all ingredients well. Coat your choice of chicken, steak or pork and grill. Also may be used as a condiment.

# CHIPPED BEEF DIP

*This great recipe is from our friend "Tater" - Lebanon, PA*

**1 pkg. chipped beef (Hormel in glass jar)**
**1-8 oz. cream cheese (Philadelphia brand) at room temperature**
**2 Tbsp. milk**
**1 cup (8 oz.) sour cream**
**¼ tsp. garlic powder or garlic salt**
**2 scallion stalks – chopped fine**
**¼ tsp. pepper**

**½ cup chopped pecans**
**2 Tbsp. butter**

Chop chipped beef rounds then combine with ingredients 1-6. Brown pecans in butter. Pour mixture into a small 1-1 ½ qt. casserole dish. Top mixture with nuts. Bake at 350° for 20 minutes. Serve with Triscuits & cocktail knives for spreading.

# ARTICHOKE DIP

*Submitted by Cousin Ann Rogers of Nassau ~ 2-11-1987*

**1 can of artichoke heads (chopped)**
**garlic salt**
**pepper**

**mayonnaise**
**garlic powder (just a little bit)**

**Parmesan Cheese (approx. ½ cup in the mix and save some for the top of the dip)**
Mix together all the above and bake at 350° until brown on top.

**No one ever says, "It's only a game," when their team is winning.**

# NOTES:

Made in the USA
Charleston, SC
22 January 2016